DON'T EXPECT the SUN TO SHINE

A Wake for Robin Blaser

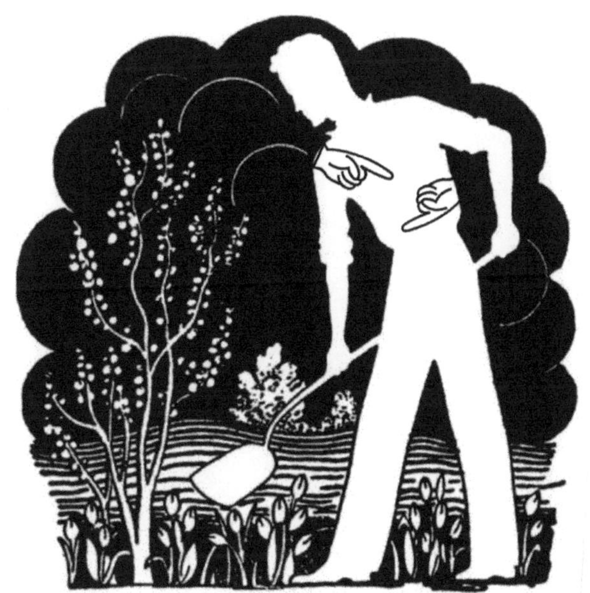

by Richard Rathwell
Staged by Harold Rhenisch

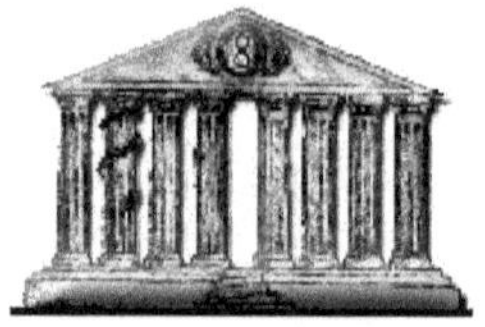

8th House Publishing
Montreal, Canada

First Edition

Published worldwide by 8th House Publishing.
Illustrations & Cover Design by Harold Rhenisch
Images under license from *The Graphics Fairy*

ISBN 978-1-926716-64-0

Designed by 8th House Publishing.
www.8thHousePublishing.com
Set in Garamond, Raleway & Grobold.

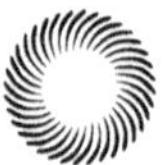

Library and Archives Canada Cataloguing in Publication

Title: Don't expect the sun to shine : a wake for Robin Blaser / by Richard Rathwell ; staged by Harold Rhenisch.
Other titles: Do not expect the sunto shine
Names: Rathwell, Richard, author. | Rhenisch, Harold, 1958- contributor.
Description: First edition. | Poems.
Identifiers: Canadiana 20220436487 | ISBN 9781926716640 (hardcover)
Classification: LCC PS8635.A84 D66 2022 | DDC C811/.6—dc23

DON'T EXPECT THE SUN TO SHINE

A WAKE FOR ROBIN BLASER

by
Richard Rathwell

Staged by
Harold Rhenisch

AN INTRODUCTION TO THE TRANSCULTURE

An Interview on a Poem as a Stage

☼ *First Session* ☼

Richard Rathwell, in your autobiography you wrote: "I have Asperger's syndrome." What is that like?

Rathwell: Asperger's Syndrome is not a disease. It can be diagnosed and called something. But so can bloodymindedness. I may not even have anything. I could just have mind.

OK, what is mind to you?

Rathwell: I can do wide loops of associated thought without reasonable connection but joined together with focussed little memory triggers. Can you?

Yes. A sagebrush. A rock by the sea. Figs.

Rathwell: A doctor may think you are Aspergers.

☼ *Second Session* ☼

You've written a book about Canadian poetry, especially the discipline of Creative Writing, centred around the wake of the poet Robin Blaser. As I read it, the book is the wake that came off poorly the first time around, but not just for Blaser. For Canada, too. Why do you feel that Canada is a corpse?

Rathwell: Canada is a land of what you'd expect, made up of mainly immigrants and descendants of immigrants, with a history of genocide.

OK, what's the memory trigger that connects all that? Most Canadians think in more linear ways. Pipelines. Rail lines. Hydroelectric transmission lines cut through Indian reservations, forests, ranches and alpine valleys.

Rathwell: Mystifying addictive fake cultures.

You'll still lose readers. Canada is certainly real. The contemporary method of dealing with any gaps in understanding is to differentiate between settler culture and Indigenous culture. Sometimes this gets confused and people talk of settlers or Indigenous people instead. Often they talk of reconciliation. Care to try again?

Rathwell: Raising hysterical issues of terrors that can't be fixed in order to divert attention from core problems is translated into poems and e-mails.

Keep going.

Rathwell: "Woke is White."

Oops. Too much too fast. Are you able to pull back a bit?

Rathwell: I get joy from the idle movement of a horse in a field of snow.

So do I. Joe Rosenblatt, wearing his poet's hat, pointed out that Canada is a chain of ten big cities along the American border, surrounded by nowhere. Could it be that the citizens of this chain have more contact with images of horses than with horses themselves?

Rathwell: Aspergers who talk and write, or dance and sing, or for that matter do anything, do not do it for the scholars and relatives who will attend their funeral.

So, it makes no difference that physical experience leaps between the gym, traffic, and a screen, usually with team sports or a brutal murder that within one hour, sometimes two, dissects innocence into heavy drinking? Aren't most of the American towns in them actual towns in Canada?

Rathwell: I am nothing.

☼ *Third Session* ☼

Richard Rathwell, I have been translating your poetry for readers for years. I have known you to be passionately committed to creating new forms for new cultural spaces that spring up where cultures blur, especially during migration or after violent attacks — spaces in which misreadings can become deadly.

Rathwell: Cultural Nationalism is deadly. Black Lives Matter and Critical Race Theory all treat oppression as something mysterious and gaseous that cannot be fixed concretely.

We're not going to win friends with that. How about we talk about my translation of the leaps in your poetry, the resonances around words, with a grammar of images and the connections between images? I mean, to get away from a culture of words surrounded by an electron haze of emotions that are sometimes particles, sometimes waves, and sometimes dancing all on its own. Can you come up with phrasing that is more inclusive?

Rathwell: The slogan of Black Lives is vampiric on emotions like bad box sets.

I get the impression that to you all words are stock phrases.

Rathwell: I am tired of those things emanating from you guys. Your structures. Except in music and math. Some of the painting. But your novels like bad fantasy games!

Because they're not concrete?

Rathwell: All woke stuff, especially the historic analytical/critical stuff, strips away dimensions of understanding and energies of revolutionary pragmatism. It is similar to the Black Nationalist Liberation movements which were hatched in U.K. universities and charitable foundations, ways of diverting attention and splitting discourse and solidarity. There is a street in Greenwich in the United Kingdom, just past the meridian on which small scale ethnic restaurants and a clubs come and go. There are often premises to rent or share, or, as the custom is here, to convert twice a month or so into a specific reorientation with permission of the present inhabitant. This is called a 'club' and it is directed to a particular target or 'tribe'. Sometimes that is a nation like Turkish food. Narcoleptic awakenings from sleep.

You're leaping again.

Rathwell: In the last few weeks, I have encountered tormented Canadian Palestinians who have written prose poems on how the United Nations causes war.

I'm sure your readers would love to hear specifics. Is it because of all the talking? Or because those white SUVs are such easy targets for anyone who has plum run out of elephant ivory?

Rathwell: We are not prepared for evolution. I cannot resist a snow poem. When the clouds rimmed the north yesterday, I opened every window to smell that cold invisibility that shoots off from under the front of it. The wedge of dirty, dry cold streaming close to the ground. The arid bloodlessness of it disturbing wet grass. Now it is here and I was in it when it began. I had hoped it would be the heavy redemptive peaceful stuff. But no, it has thunder in it somewhere. It has developed like pumice. Get it?

So, both the talking and the SUVs?

Rathwell: What I really want is cross-fertilization, the breaking down of enclosing narratives and the celebration of breaking out. When sufis swirl, they negate negation.

☼ *Fourth Session* ☼

In my effort to translate your Aspergers, I have used images to make your leaps and resonances into connections and gestures, while allowing your texts to be as they always were, a kind of narrative running as a horse through the grass. Have you always had multiple narratives loping through your experience?

Rathwell: I am a revolutionary pragmatist.

Do you mean what an editor once told me, that a new form rises from a need to say something that couldn't be said in any other way?

Rathwell: Divide by dissonance prevails.

Like Putin in the Ukraine? Or Lutoshenko on the Polish border? Or both of them together?

Rathwell: In literature you get victim literature, which diverts from realism.

Realism? Do you mean Madame Bovary, who got confused by books? Or Anna Karenina, who got tangled in train timetables? Or that other 19th century novelist, Margaret Atwood, who invented a prosthesis?

Rathwell: It is amazing how you consider only silently that somehow guilt is shared. You have left out Yahweh. I am.

Good catch. But a name that means "I am", "I was" and "I will be," isn't that the same as saying "I is," wherever you are? Could this compression of ambiguity be the opposite of transculture?

Rathwell: I am the negation they negate.

I suspect you mean that in an urban culture, you, any identity self, are the streets and houses transcultural actors move through? Would it follow that literature is the way a street is surfaced, with asphalt, with bricks, with dust, with mud, with or without dogs or feces, with or without rape, automobiles, synagogues, shell holes or people? That some of its people are biological, others are mechanical, and some are images sprayed onto walls. Very popular and much fought over. Often a prey site. In Canada, cities hire people to remove art from building walls. Shall we begin with that?

Rathwell: A pragmatist is something deploying one's material person in interaction with a real world.

I'll take that as a tentative yes. I do note that you refer to yourself, the am of your I, as a thing, and not a body. Have you always thought of your thingness as your self and your self as distinct from your bodily experience?

Rathwell: The Bantu can say I am you; I am not you. On the same river. Changing consonants. Singing vowels differently.

Is this disassociation part of Aspergers or part of how Aspergers is read in Canadian culture? Or is it not Aspergers at all?

Rathwell: The same Gods are different in different places.

There are land mines on many of the passes. That kind of thing?

Rathwell: God spoke Arabic.

☼ *Fifth Session* ☼

Thinking of the fields of meaning around your words, what for a non-Aspergers might be called emotional relevance, or feeling, would it be fair to say that in "Don't Expect the Sun to Shine" you write a script for any of the vast number of self-replicating and self-generating amalgams of technology, surface and embodiment that produce the country's literature?

Rathwell: In literature, the transculturalists and revolutionary pragmatists were killed.

As they are in TV detective shows? Are those wakes, too?

Rathwell: Globalization progresses.

Fair enough. Given that even the CBC considers poetry to be stories, often laid out like parking lot crashes, how about we say: Rathwell provides a guide to the country that was and a script for navigating the post-national space it inhabits now? You present Canada as a field into which American literatures plow and British literatures sow their stories, regardless of its gender. What is it by itself?

Rathwell: The sinister opportunists of false ferocity and side-line slogan-shouting, icon smearing, and statue toppling.

So, much the same thing. A friend told me yesterday that there was no point toppling statues of Karl Marx after the fall of communism in the German East, because Marx wasn't a communist. Then she attacked her water-logged sub-floor with a hammer and a chisel. Have you thought of how these new Marxists, the ones not of economics but of bodily identities, will take to that?

Rathwell: The Solictor General of Canada once called me the country's greatest terrorist threat. I once spent weeks planning how to blow up the 18th hole at the UBC Golf Course. A hole. Their fate is yet to be determined this side of eternity.

They will see themselves as creating it.

Rathwell: As with all identities assumed or inherent floating outside person-made structures.

OK, let's go with this, then: Rathwell's lens is their literature, the manner in which a human inhabits the dwelling places of words, passes them on to others, or uses them to control others at a distance. He states that his goal is to disrupt how they use this dwelling to transform revolution into fear.

Rathwell: A fix for racism requires a complete rejigging of systems and the seizing of the instruments of culture.

☼ *Sixth Session* ☼

Mr. Rathwell, in "Don't Expect the Sun to Shine" you criticize poets for concentrating on being heads of English Departments, one after the other, while asking if you are "back." If they had chosen to become the arms of English Departments, or their legs or ears, would you have been more openly critical, or less so?

Rathwell: My university suspended me. The secret police unemployed me, the terror squad beat me. If writing is an avocation with purpose then it must ignite useful imagination. And destroy useless. They achieve their own vision of coronation and enthronement. I am not "back."

I'm sorry for your loss. I presume you mean they came to the wake as representatives of institutions, while you came because you loved the poet?

Rathwell: Hardly anyone came. The food was stolen by a homeless person in the alley!

So, the *event* was literature.

Rathwell: Only a couple of us went into the living room to view the body.

If I follow you, in 2009 you had already noticed that literature in Canada was uninhabited, except by a corpse?

Rathwell: Revolution turns things around.

You say you live in London, when you are not in France. Does this perspective as a Canadian in the world, rather than in Canada, create your book as a turning around? Are you looking behind you, over your shoulder, so to speak? Are you being followed? I presume by jackals?

Rathwell: Revolutionary pragmatism is the projection of the imagination (and intellect) into morbid 'can't be fixed so scream and moan' diabolic creature generation of single dimension thought machinery of the cycles of capitalism.

Language as a complete series of leaps! Nouns and verbs losing their differentiation. Is that the revolution?

Rathwell: I am nothing.

Do you not mean "I" is nothing?

Rathwell: How else are you to describe it? I did not invent transculturalism. Rather, I am trying to give meaning to it. As I tried with communism but failed.

Statue toppling, then?

Rathwell: It is when cultures collide. Then you have attempts at new connections, in new fields.

☼ *Seventh Session* ☼

Mr. Rathwell, let me give it a try: Revolutionary pragmatism is a term for the projection of imagination and intellect into cultural machinery. It describes the act of putting some life into frozen emotional states created by cultural structures beyond the capacity of any one person to change. How's that?

Rathwell: I don't exist. There are parables, too. Two for one.

I'm intrigued. What parables?

Rathwell: There is fear and death. Piccadilly is closed at one side for the runaways to sit on, writing angry poems and giving materiality to their fears as they are cruised. So, off you go.

Perhaps it is meant to give them character.

Rathwell: Real people have no character. Only characters have character.

Plus, I'd say there are the selves created by this sense of being trapped. You call those "morbid, diabolic creatures." Do you mean zombies?

Rathwell: The slogan of Black Lives Matter is not only meaningless but divisive of magnifiers of support. Conflict often is a reoccurrence of previous contradictions expressed in new forms.

But not communication?

Rathwell: All woke stuff, especially the historic analytical/critical stuff, strips away dimensions of understanding.

But doesn't it give new ones, as you say? Couldn't we say *after* Christian tradition there are Walmart greeters and hydroelectric transmission lines marching across 1,000 kilometres of the British Columbia mountains, with the forests beneath them kept clear by herbicides and summer forestry students with metal-bladed weed whackers hung on their hips like penises with rotary teeth?

Rathwell: Who took up arms (real ones) against colonialism? As well as taught peasant revolutionaries to read (manuals)? Who made sure Zimbabwean Historic Narratives made sense in the new history books?

Nobody?

Rathwell: I am nobody.

☼ *Eighth Session* ☼

Mr. Rathwell, I've staged your texts for the paper screen, translated into scripts for biological memories. I thought it would be a way to represent selves being led to the Polish-Belarussian border and turned into armaments, or left abandoned in Kabul after the film crews have flown off. Would you say that this is the transculture?

Rathwell: I am a fable.

Yes, interbreeding is common. In the time of the transculture, a space of fluid energy flows between the earth and virtual identity.

Rathwell: Like that other newer, better friend phoning from the dead about something I didn't understand.

Exactly! Many forces are seeking to replace us. Your car, for instance. Your toaster. I include some of these in the text to deflect its control. We should put them on notice.

Rathwell: All philosophy is eviscerated in shivering. All words exist without intention. Higher things deflated, nude, within a dressing gown of faded mystery. One wants flesh to be as healthy as possible. Poetry is invisible in ordinary life.

But still present? Where would I look for some of this stuff?

Rathwell: In speech, silence and memory. It can be something else previously unimaginable.

Unimaginable and yet, like my visual stagings of the radio signals for which your poems are broadcast antennae, present. Did you write the words intentionally as scripts for performance? I mean, is life a drama?

Rathwell: I was once, in my world, the smartest guy in the seminar, the coolest at the party, the bravest and most cunning in work. As I became stupider, I understood this. It is a kind of dust to dust, ashes to ashes thing, but taking into account where those god damn ashes came from.

Yahweh eating grasshoppers with John Lennon in a little joint in The Village while drawing the first design sketches for John the Baptist on the back of a napkin? With communication going in all directions at once?

Rathwell: I was creation. In my imagination I would conquer the world immediately, in the future after death. Not just in a fury of bubbles but in ferocious vengeance.

John's wife Yoko reacted to the bullets by building an artificial, white Aurora above Reykjavik every winter.

Rathwell: Fortunately I did not.

☼ *Ninth Session* ☼

Mr. Rathwell, in "Don't Expect the Sun to Shine", you mention that living culture is like a vivid dream. What do you mean by this "like"? Currently, culture is kept in line because there are people who direct traffic. Sometimes with truncheons. Sometimes with white silk gloves. Sometimes with people marching arm in arm, kept apart by people marching arm in arm down cross streets, who are kept back by police in face shields. You need a permit for this.

Rathwell: They are shallow rooted as the Spanish Grass waving over snow, attempting procreation uselessly in the cold outside. In the wind. Something even the last park dogs are avoiding.

Sure, but let's say there is poetry in "it", or novels. Let's say that "the" culture is arranged in such a way that every poet is asked to give the inciting incident of their poem and to describe "its" theme. Let's say that "the culture" is arranged in such a way that the form of every one of the "the poems" makes the same assumptions and thus, because poems are formal objects, even ceremonial objects of address, says precisely the same thing. Is this kind of internalized CBC what you mean when you say "even truth can be critiqued"?

Rathwell: A coffin surely. Or just a face in glass. My country of memory is all anecdote and no myth. All flakes and no blizzard.

It can be fictions in this culture. There always are.

Rathwell: I grow weary of conversations with ghosts.

Because they're not in the transculture, and so are fading away, increasingly invisible to anyone who is?

Rathwell: All accent and no language. All text.

Like old communist intellectuals stepping out of a football crowd in Weimar, Germany, when I started photographing Nazi graffiti after I rattled on the Modern Art Gallery's unexpectedly locked door, catching my eye, dismissing me, and then melting back into the crowd and vanishing?

Rathwell: Once the eye filled the blank spots, the ear the silences. Once there was a boundary between seeing and feeling and thinking and saying and having a theory of the dead. We all remain better than our reputations, but who remembers?

Perhaps our staging of your text is memory, as an active force.

Rathwell: I am happy I have failed at it with increasing expertise.

☼ *Tenth Session* ☼

Mr. Rathwell, by definition and agreement, a fiction is a story, with characters, symbolism, things lifted from "reality", things made up, sentences, conflict, rising action, motifs, description and clunky bits of narrative, and sometimes streets, dogs, mangoes, money passing hands, rarely poetry, often villains, once in a while humour, and always a fictioneer, asked to explain the motivations of their characters to a radio audience driving to or from a warehouse grocery store to buy mangoes, or peppers, rarely vaccines, and never rape or feces. By convention, it is accepted that these stories tell truth by telling lies. Life becomes a springboard. Is it like that for you, too?

Rathwell: As a temporary collection of chemicals conducting sensory memory disappears traceless as the frozen grass is now gone in lightless snow.

Let's say it is so, then. Many of Canadian culture's fictions are, understandably, set in fictional worlds, often with fantastical creatures or a bush full of ghosts or spies taking down gun runners. Let's say that they are T-shirts that are donated to the poor in Canada, sorted in warehouses in Mississauga, baled and sent through the St. Lawrence River locks to Africa. Let's say that after a cold trip across the Atlantic, they are unpacked among dogs and offer people the chance to wear advertisements for Tire Shops in Moose Jaw, a donut joint in Hamilton or a bottle of screech from a visit to the Vikings, now dead and gone, in an old fishing station without fish called Newfoundland although it has been forgotten, as fill-ins for television sit-coms, reality shoes and TSN. Have you worn shirts like that, in Egypt, maybe? Or Nigeria?

Rathwell: Multiculturalism never got beyond smokescreen politics. There is no need to write down memories and burn them in the gas fire behind me, permanent with fireproof coals.

Let's say there *is* a revolution. Could we then say that there is a thing called capitalism, that people can be bought and sold or rendered obsolete, depreciated, written off, claimed as an expense over future earnings, and transformed into a junk bond sold to the Irish and turned back into profit at a loss?

Rathwell: My love dissolved like burning papers into flickering gestures.

Let's say that this is impractical. Let's say that there is something that can be done. Let's say that the first step is to be nobody, then nothing, then a wind blowing down a street, emptying and filling it at once.

Rathwell: Did I write it?

Did "I" illustrate it?

☼ *Eleventh Session* ☼

Mr. Rathwell, let's say that there is more nothing in the world than there is something but that some things are trying to hijack a revolution. Let's say that rather than the life that generates out of nothing, it combines planks, boards, nails and over-turned busses into barricades, that it makes things. Let's say that it asks only that language be simplified into a tool that can say something but never nothing, so that it can be transferred to things. Does this leave people to be its tattoos stamped on the world?

Rathwell: Stalin, Hitler and Mao on culture. Read them. They are foundations of modern interculturalism and multiculturalism, the politics of modern diversity and inclusionisms, as the post-colonial nation rah rahs for thieves under the banners of public service and community, memoir and entitlement, as victims, al three modernists on culture saying only the pure heritage, the authentic real thing, me, will survive or none will.

There are people who are concerned about these things. They have come to see that there are people who walk among these tattoos, invisibly. Let's say that there are people who want to address the instructors of this craft. Let's say that they are not hidden.

Rathwell: The theory of memory provides means whereby those who can't get it can get it by providing images for them to sequence. Practitioners are distinct from academics. Their research is distinct in that it is for creation. Their point of view is distinct, as it is not detached from emotion, landscape and imagination, except as a device of language to create image and thought.

So, Yahweh is a practitioner?

Rathwell: Practitioners teach and learn as practitioners. Practitioners are not on the side-lines or from elsewhere. They are in writing.

That writing is an active process and once it is done, it makes its readers into the written?

Rathwell: This experience indicates that many paradigms in which writing, publishing and critique thrived have now lost energy, indeed any possibility, for uncritical belief. They cannot elicit a desired reader response. For example, Eurocentric decolonization has not worked as a basis for cultural projects which sustain an enabling and critical imaginative atmosphere. Nationalism, Pan Africanism, Globalization and the attitudes of the Postmodern and Post-colonial have not yet provided, if they ever can, liberating paradigms for the human imagination that can be applied to the human condition.

Is this condition not a ghost generated by the approach of a human body to the unfolding narrative of language encoded on a page? What dimensions does this condition take on, now that the paradigm of the book is dead and every page is now a multidimensional screen?

Rathwell: Neuroscience on the flexibility of the brain can get people out of stereotypes, holes and paradigms entrenched in neuro-patterns by rewarding the brain with images to link up in new ways and keeping the paradigm out of it.

The screen is alive. Every page is now a book.

Rathwell: I found it is not hard to think of others.

Let's say there is a culture.

Harold Rhenisch with Richard Rathwell

November 2021

DON'T EXPECT THE SUN TO SHINE

A Wake for Robin Blaser

by Richard Rathwell
Staged by Harold Rhenisch

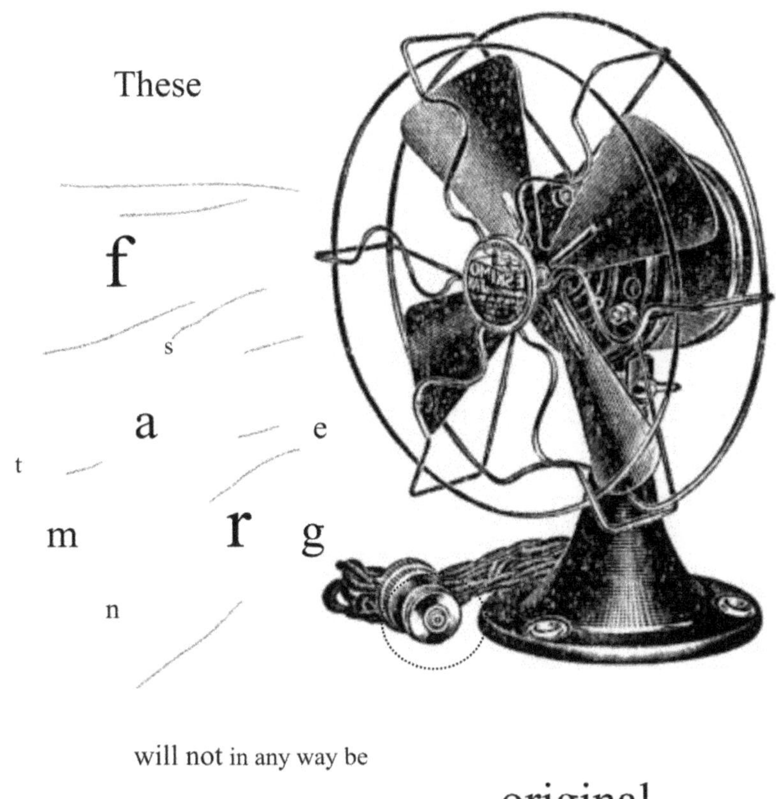

These

f

s

a e

t

m r g

n

will not in any way be

original

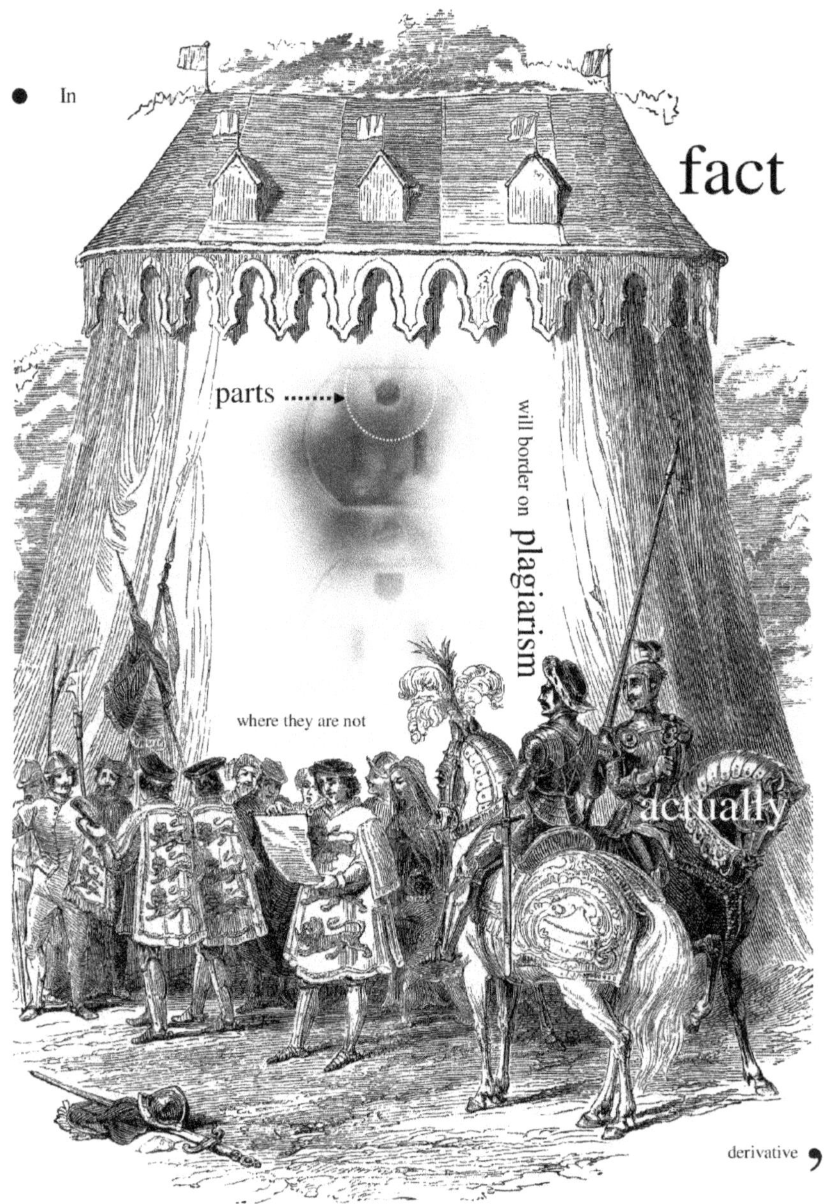
• In
fact
parts
will border on plagiarism
where they are not
actually
derivative ,

for that is the way culture is lived ~~livid~~ lived.

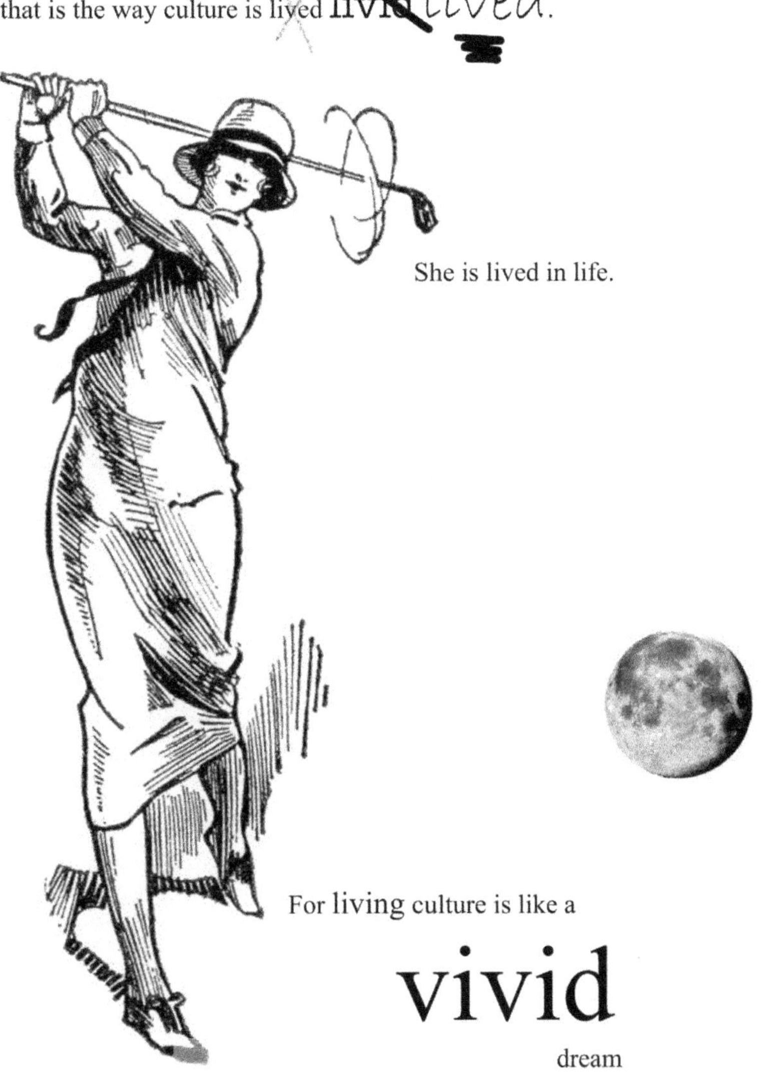

She is lived in life.

For living culture is like a

vivid

dream

That is the sort of dream that differs from an ordinary one
in that one realizes at some point one is dreaming.

and tries to **influence**

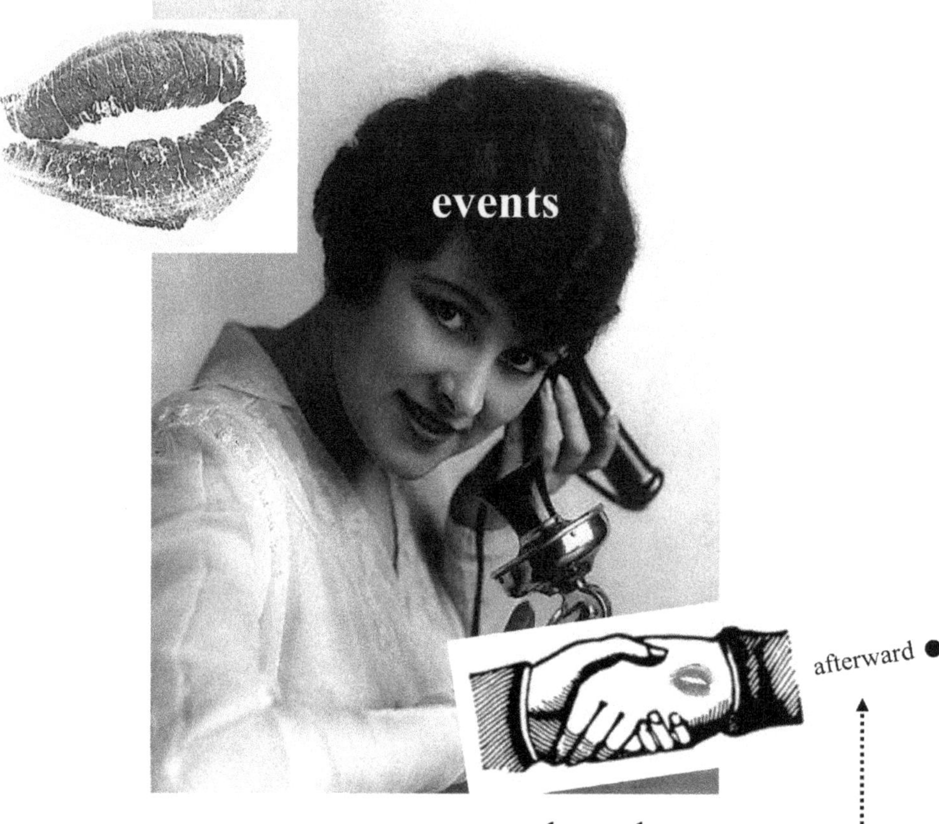

afterward •

An ordinary dream is only remembered.

Some of the detail is therefore recollected

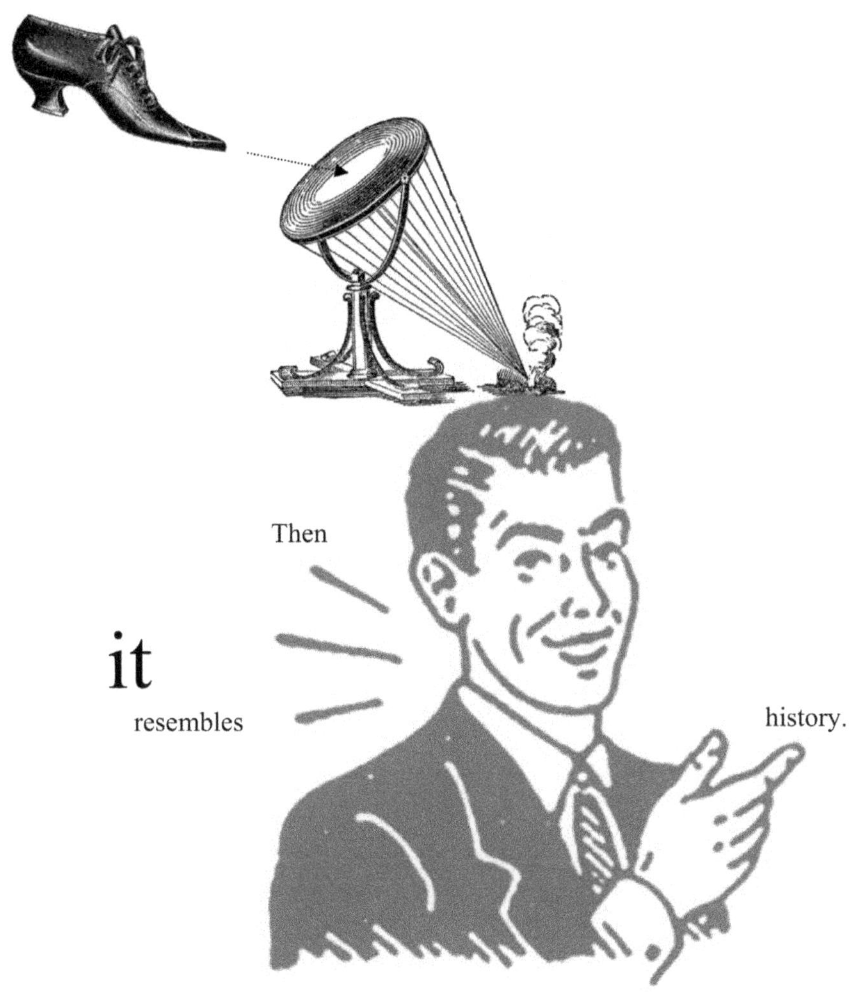
Then
it
resembles
history.

In that:

☒ the memory is falsely reorganized
☒ with a narrative fantasy to project a partisan image
☐ for the record.

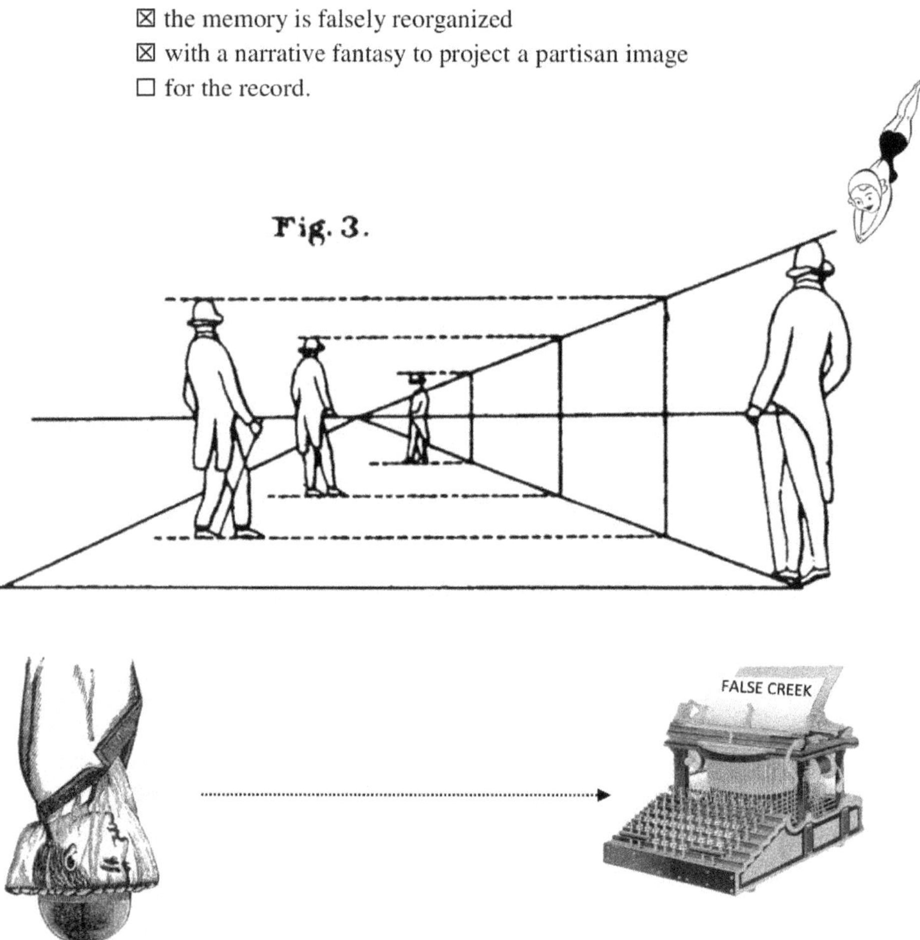

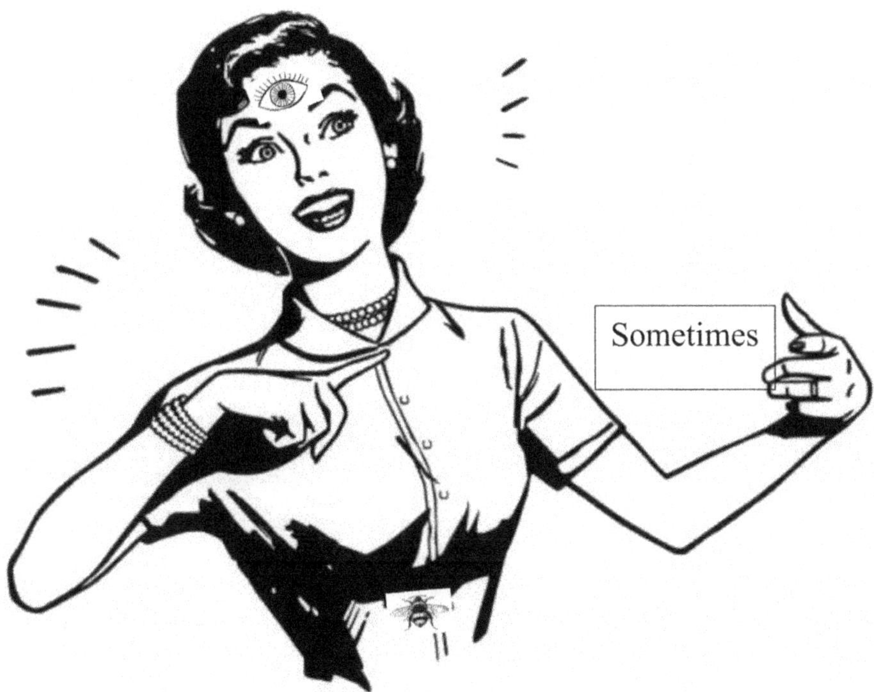

the dream goes further

to delusion

when one is awake.

Like the sleeping dream
or dead culture

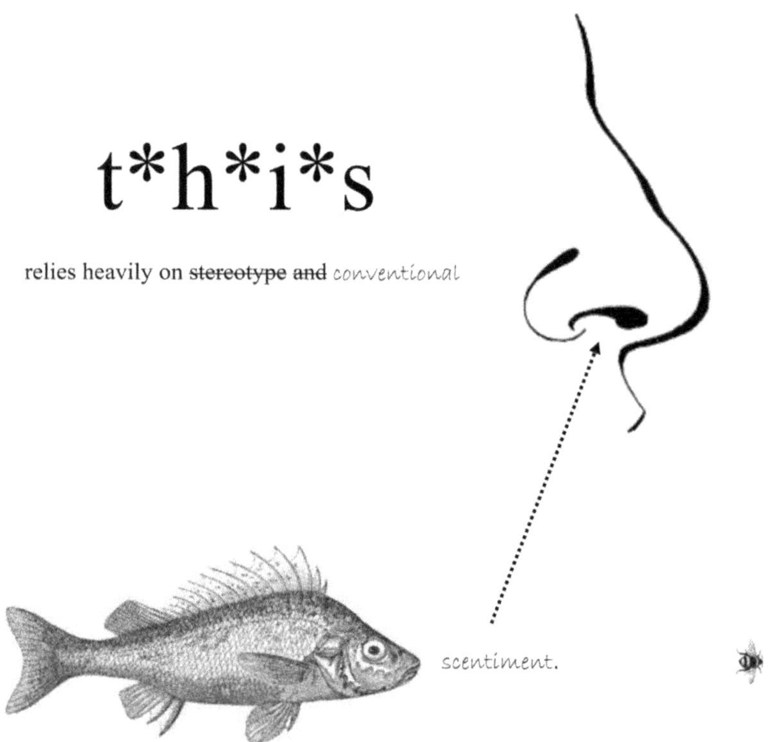

t*h*i*s

relies heavily on ~~stereotype and~~ conventional

scentiment.

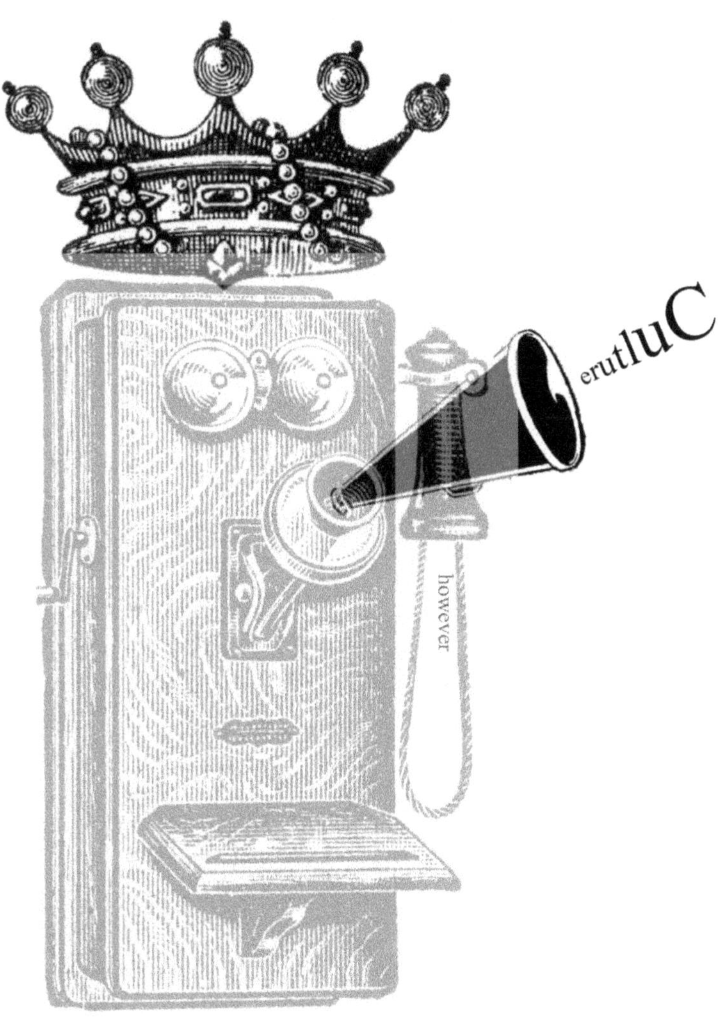
erutluC
however

,

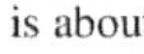

is about

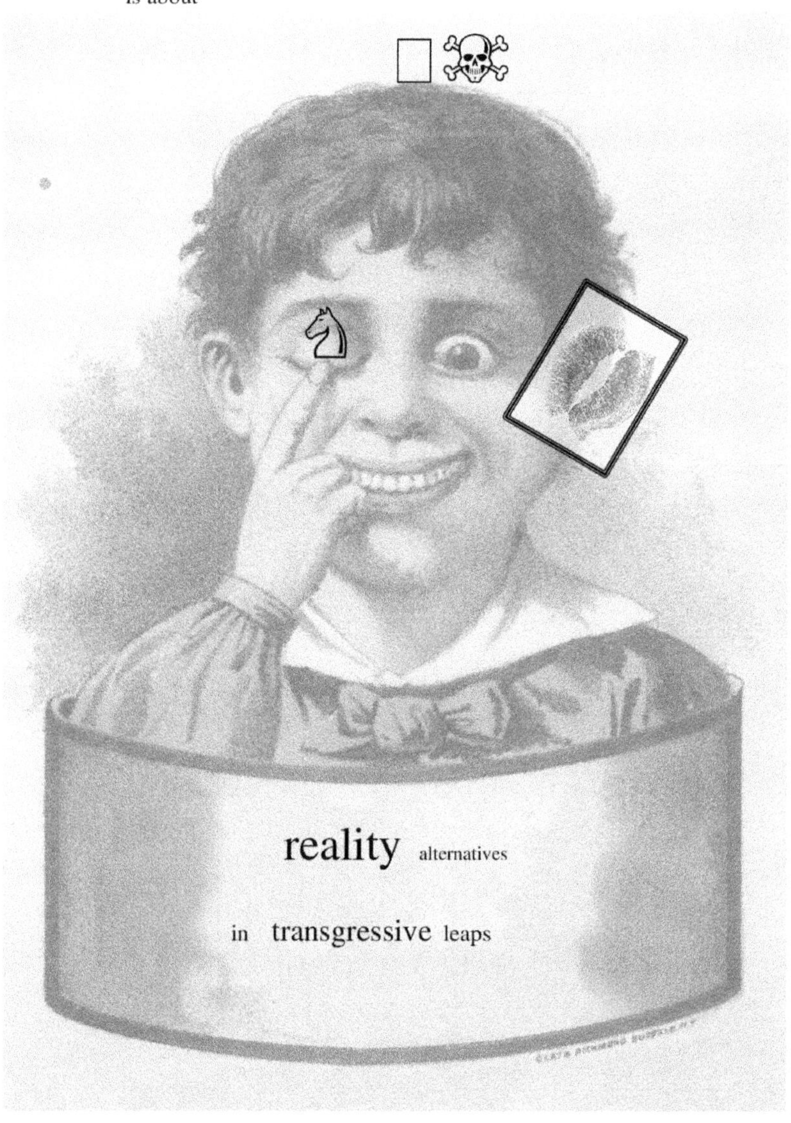

against all dreaming.

There is a science developing about

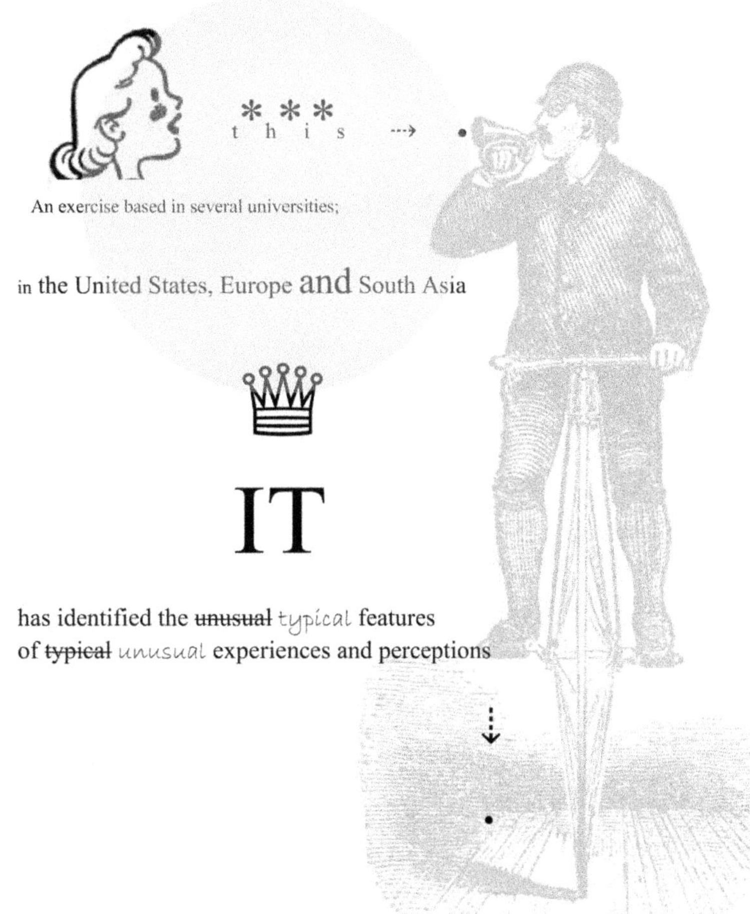

An exercise based in several universities;

in the United States, Europe and South Asia

IT

has identified the ~~unusual~~ *typical* features
of ~~typical~~ *unusual* experiences and perceptions

The exercise began with several projects
to filter out

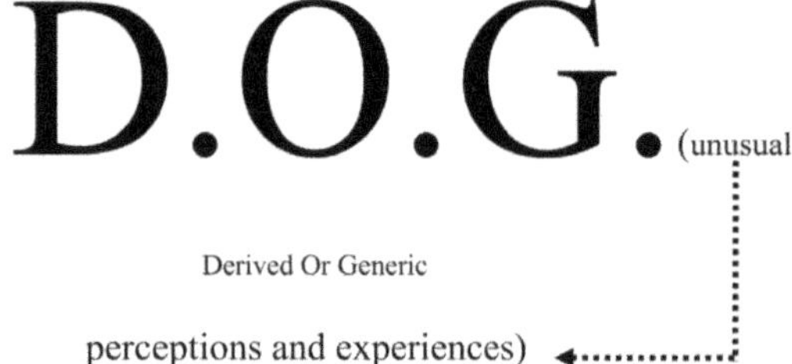

in a ~~very really extremelely~~ very large

S.O.P.

Segment of the Populations.

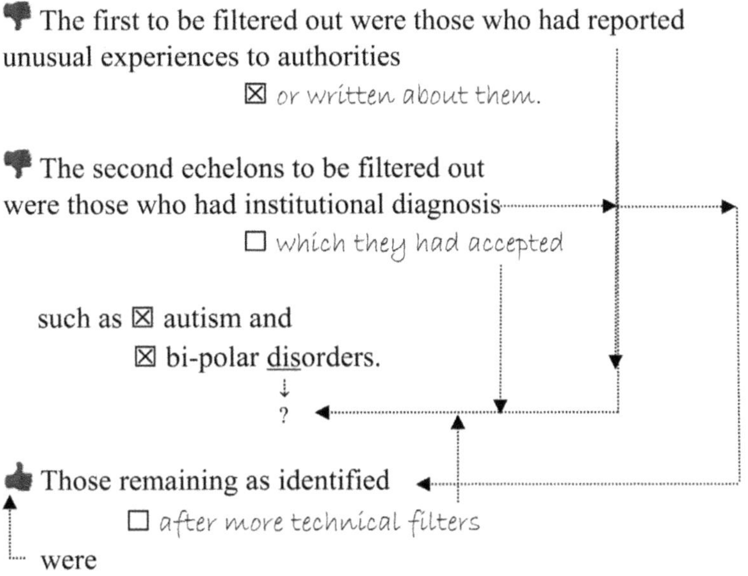
The first to be filtered out were those who had reported unusual experiences to authorities
☒ or written about them.
The second echelons to be filtered out were those who had institutional diagnosis
☐ which they had accepted
such as ☒ autism and
☒ bi-polar disorders.
?
Those remaining as identified
☐ after more technical filters
were

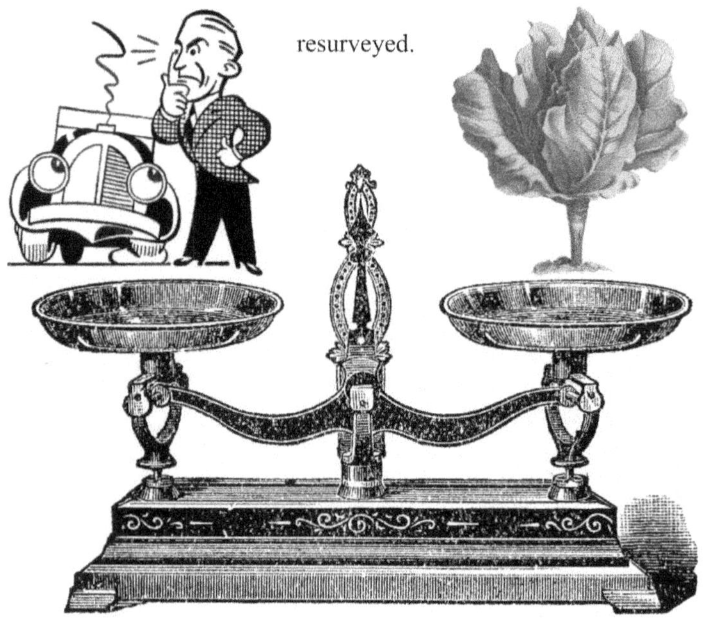
resurveyed.

In order to produce a catalogue
of the essential features of such experiences,

This was done

within the confines of a much larger social and economic inquiry

After the essential features were filtered out
the catalogue items were taken back
to other parts of the population
to see if they were familiar.

The experiences catalogued as

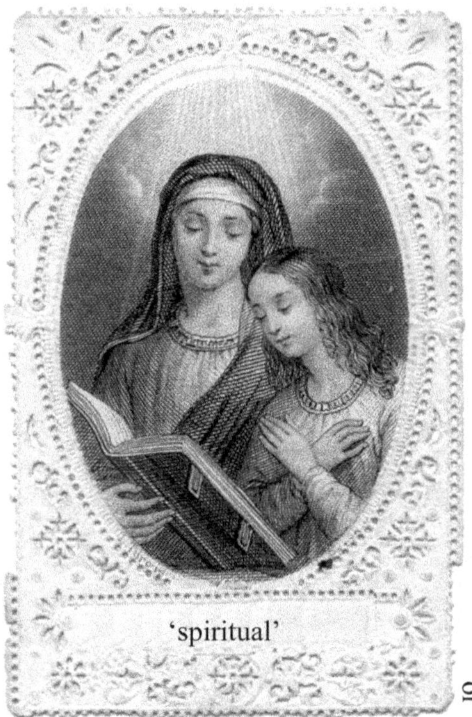

or

W. A. R.

'weird and real,

but I don't want anyone to know'

had features which have been roughly paralleled
in my series of prose pieces
which I considered to be written
so as to be authorial

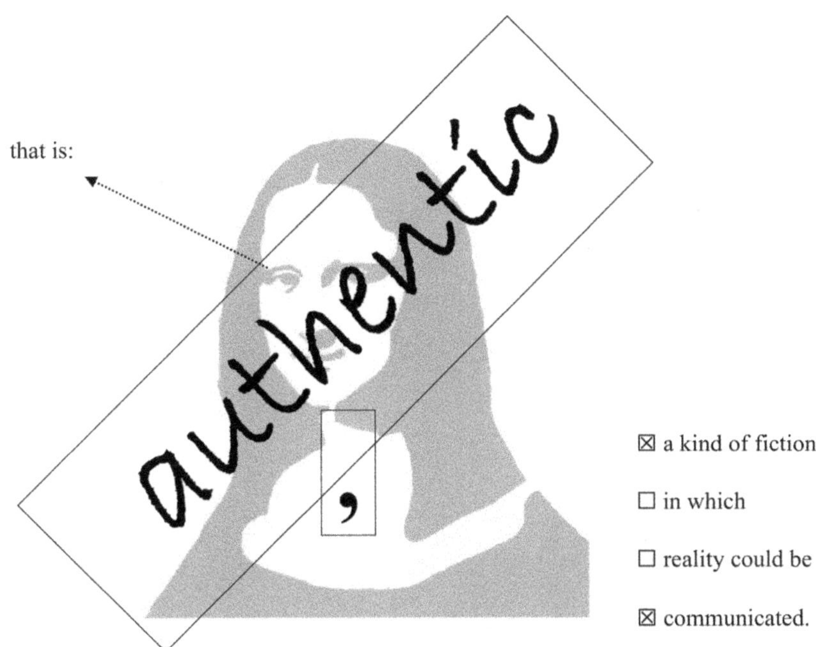

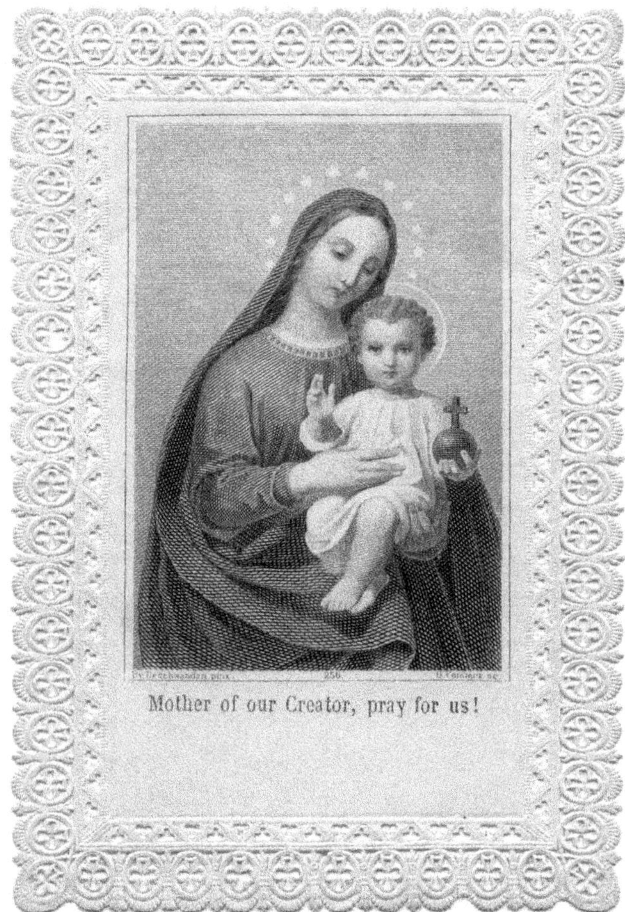

This ~~riting~~ ~~righting~~ writing

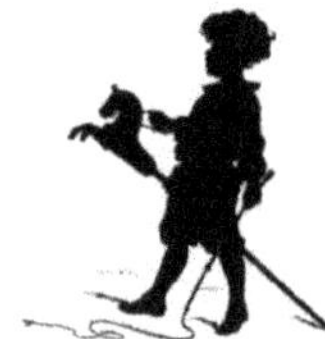

I thought

was a good alternative to the type of:

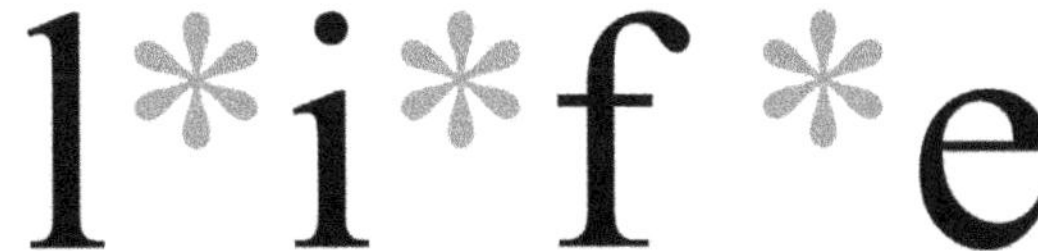

lived as a fiction so one could feel

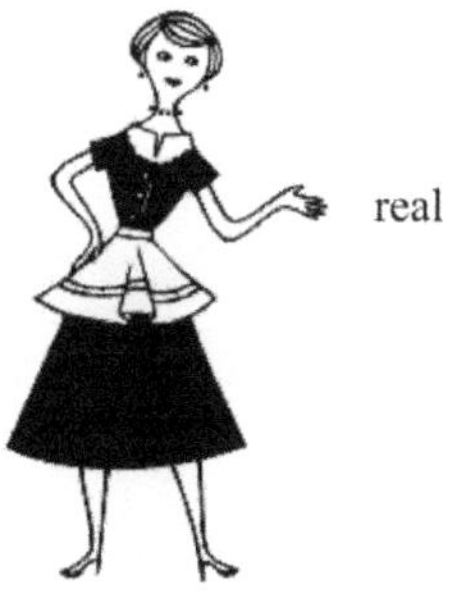

real

👍 One essential was a feeling of dislocation.
👎 This was supplemented by losses in linear
and measured

time.

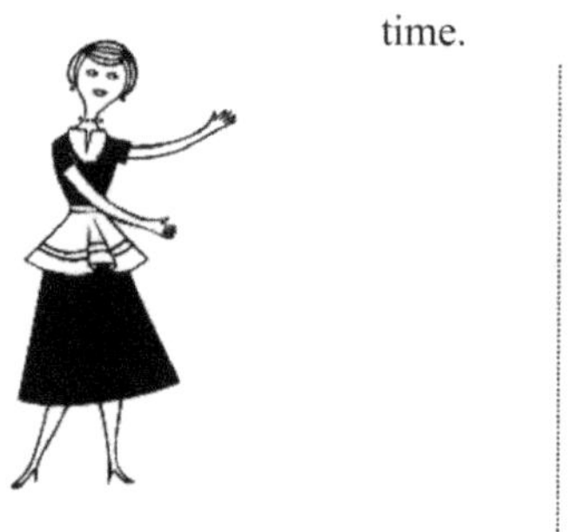

That ⇢ takes ⇢ place ⇢ in ⇢ a ⇢ repetitive ⇢ scenario ⇢ involving ⇢ rivers ⇢ and ⇢ caves

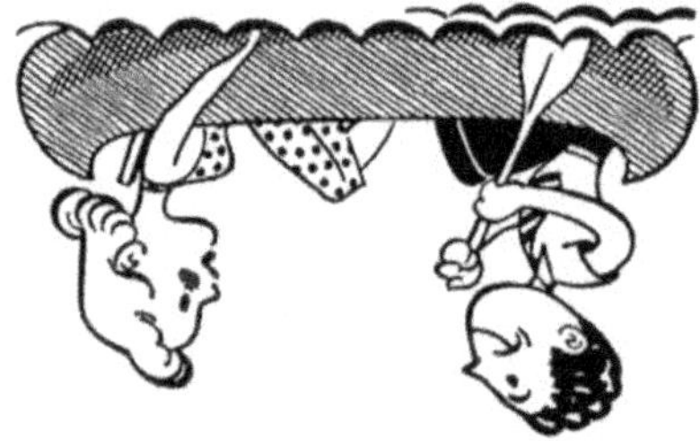

or

big buildings.

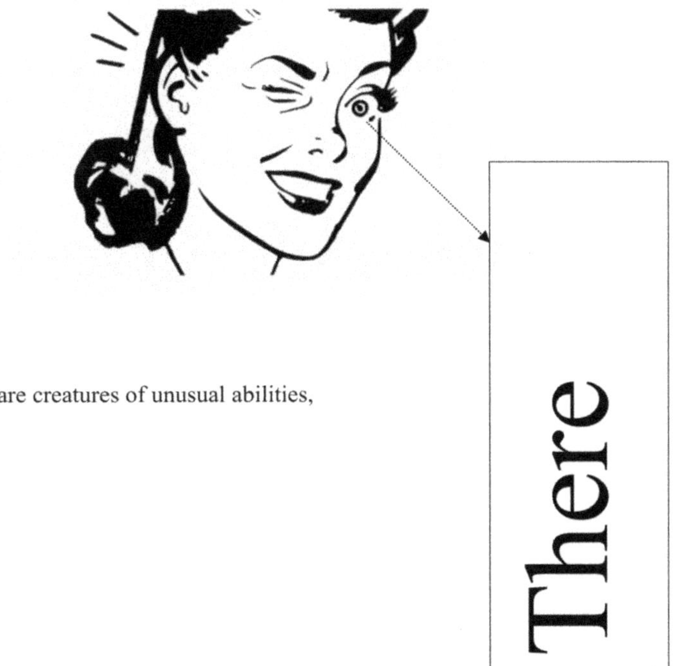

There

are creatures of unusual abilities,

including person-seeming ones.

In: the survey the latter were represented in
a drawing which combined the attributes
witnessed by those surveyed

rendered typical.

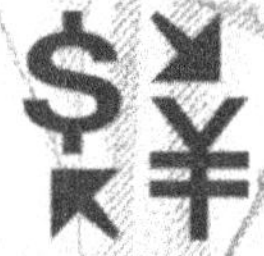

Small children

who saw these
shown amongst other ones of cartoons and monsters

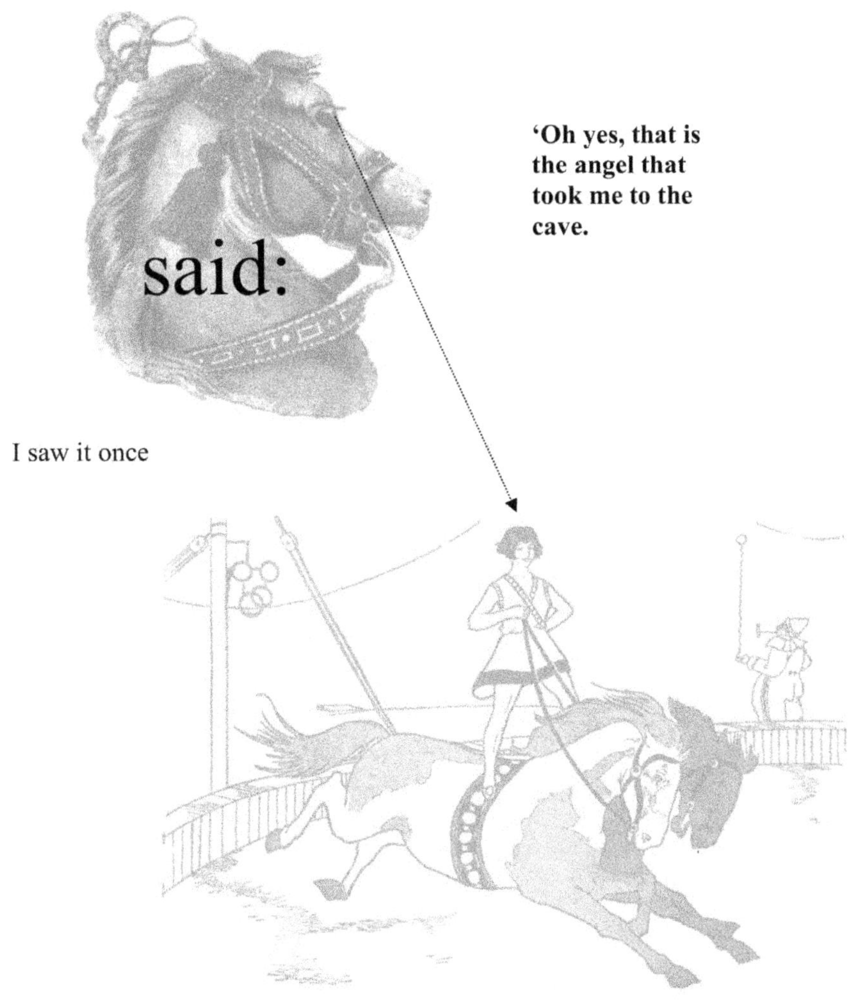

said:

'Oh yes, that is the angel that took me to the cave.

I saw it once

and it was exactly that woman.'

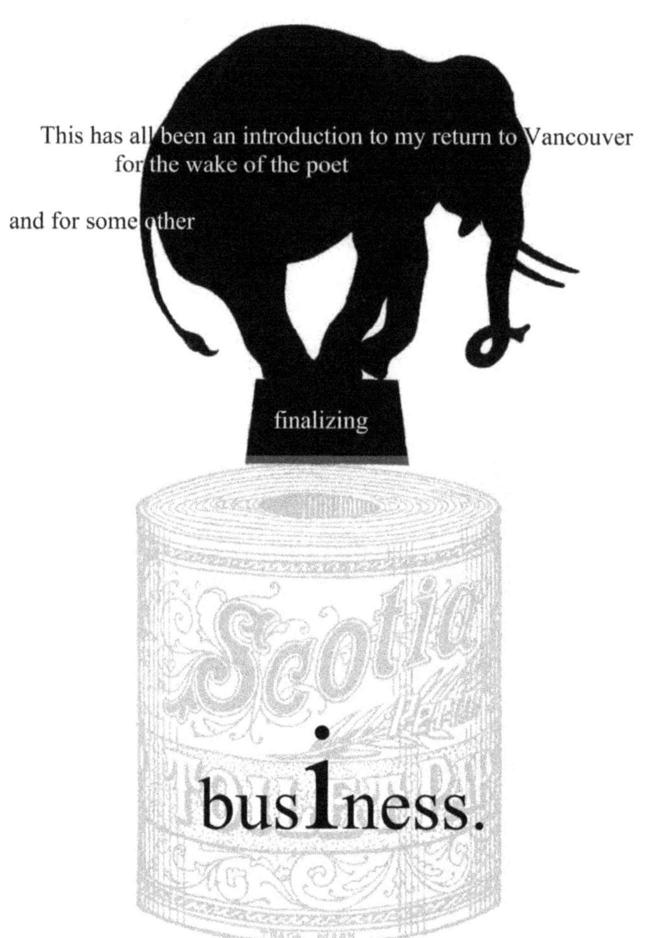

This has all been an introduction to my return to Vancouver
for the wake of the poet

and for some other

finalizing

business.

He

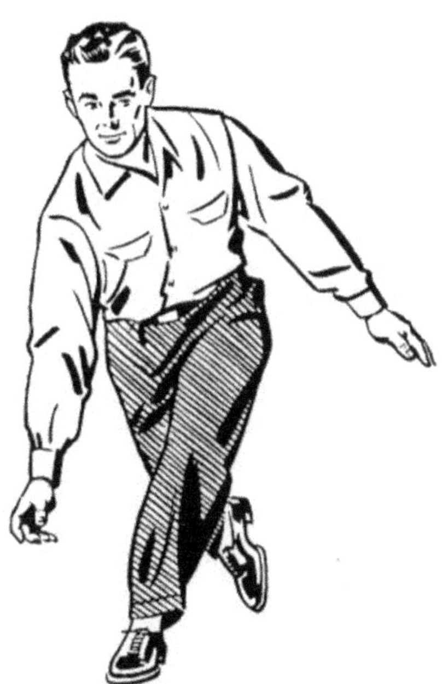

would be made historical as a significant poet
of a certain group & attitude
and was to be remembered as

a *g*r*e*a*t* teacher.

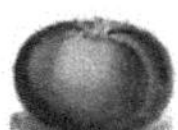

As I stepped

d

o into

the

w

garden

n

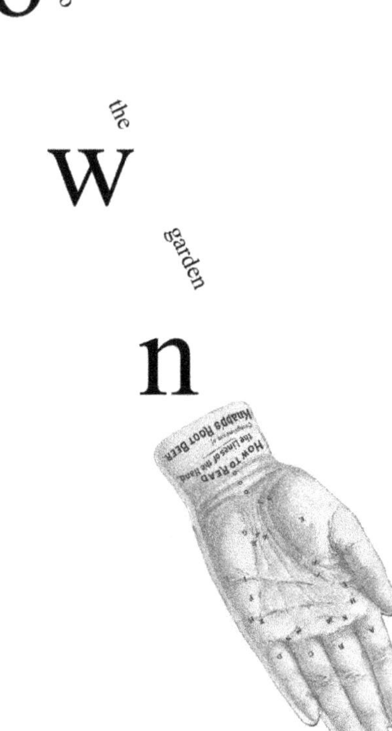

where the wake had been catered,

As it was **only** friends and colleagues
gathered together

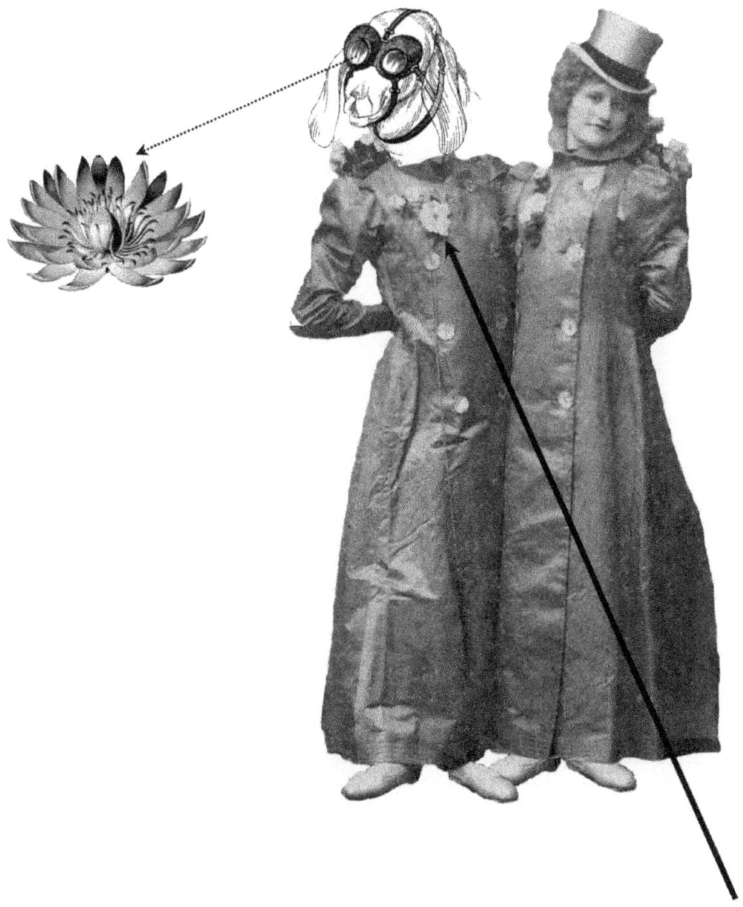

As I heard a voice asking if the poet was **there**,

AS

I saw the sunken garden as a box of dung beetles,
those that have pieces of glass pasted on their backs

but without the balls of dung

which when pushed around made them:

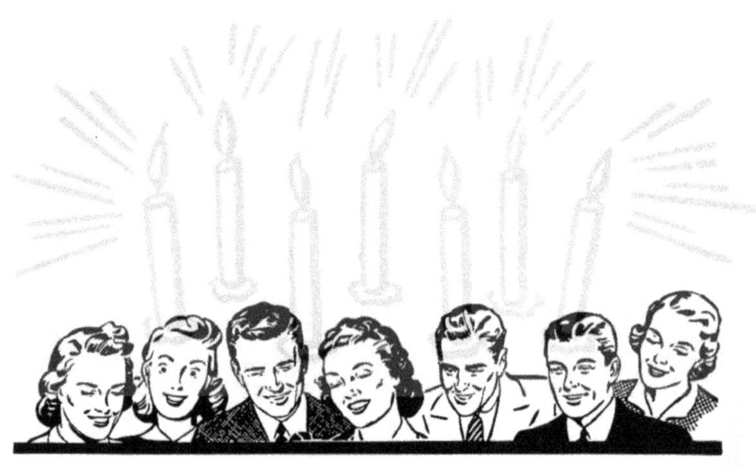

symbols of the eternal,

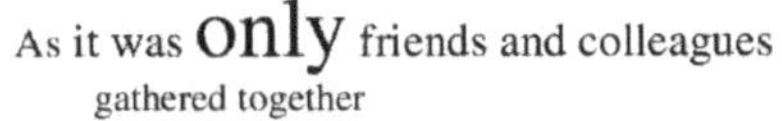

As it was only friends and colleagues
gathered together
As they had done on many occasions
over the last thirty years

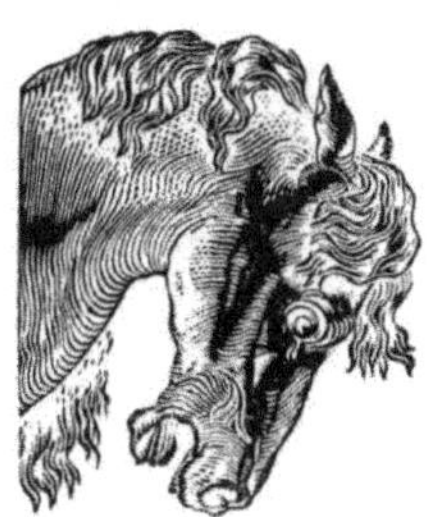

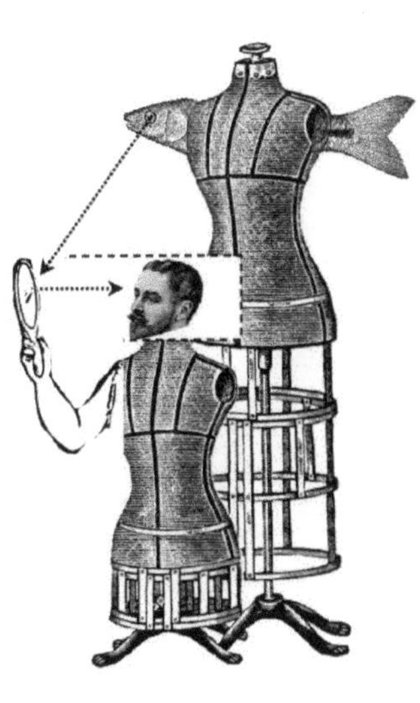

I had not been there,

Having such a vision

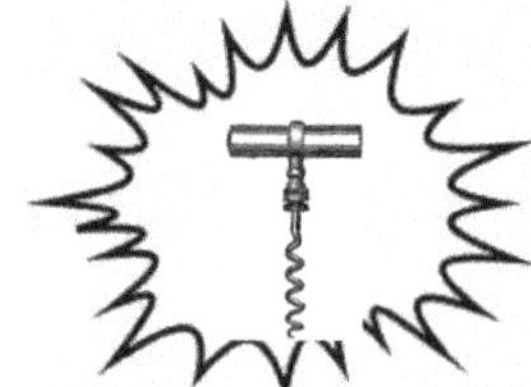

for me

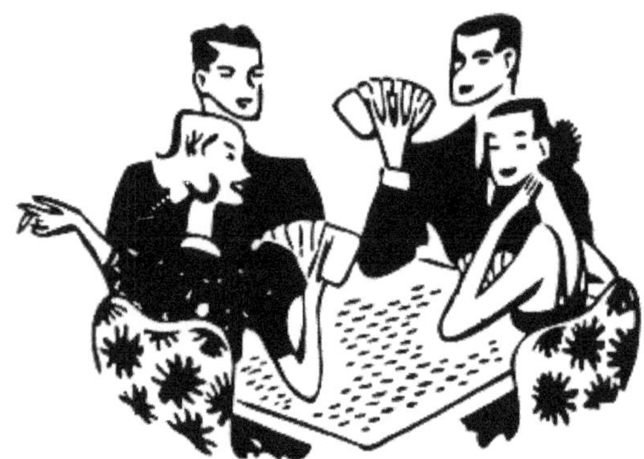

was not an *un*usual occurrence

but

being at a gathering where the placement
and personalities

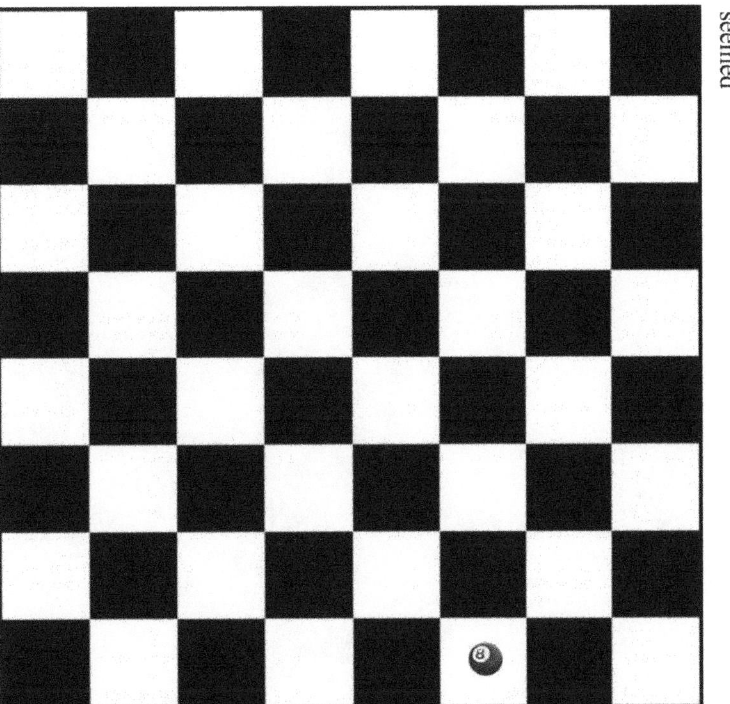

seemed

unchanged from the last time

over such a period

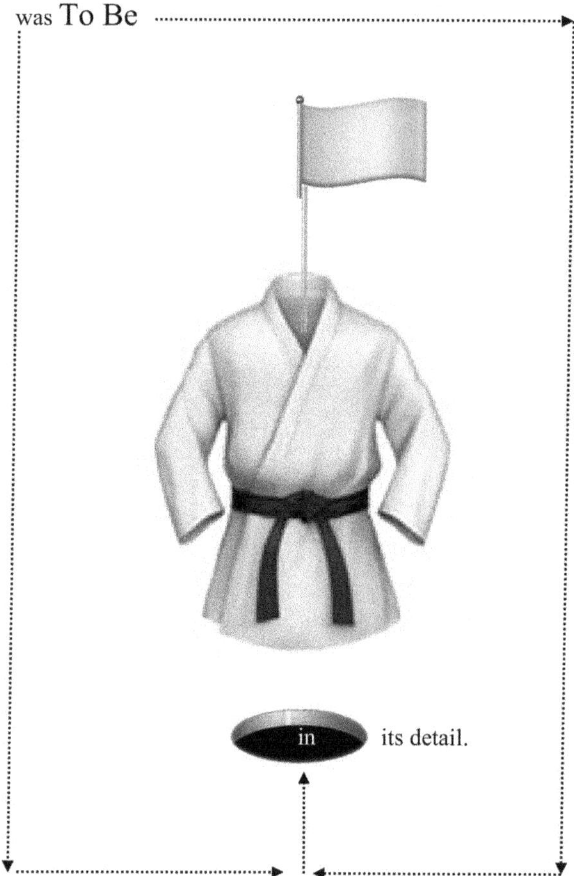
was To Be
in
its detail.

And a

v*o*i*c*e

answered:

He is there in the living room !

of the house !

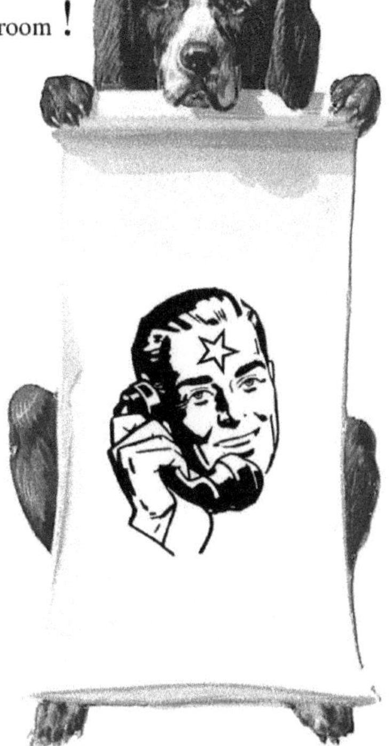

and seems rather stern !

from one angle

I

appreciated the specificity
and glittering particularism

of that

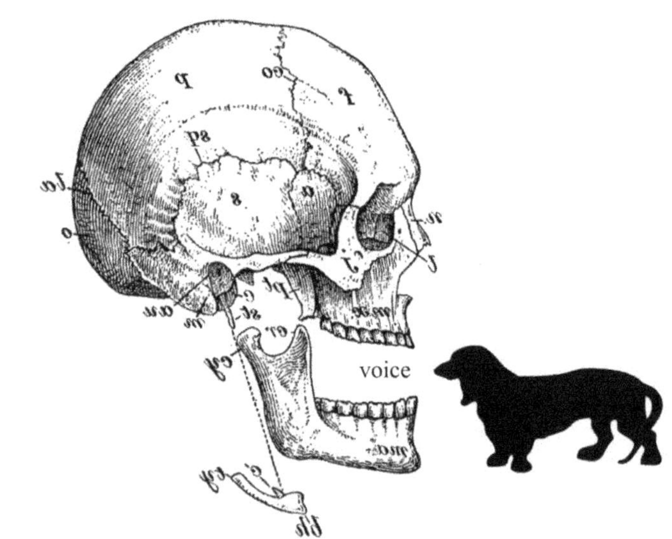

voice

in tune with the aesthetic espoused
from those

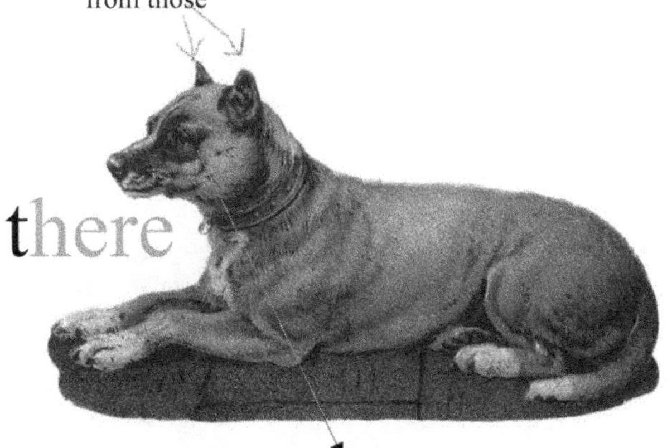

there

,

now mainly late style poets and

entrenched

academics

,

with former prize pupils and mid-term lovers of the circle,
or both

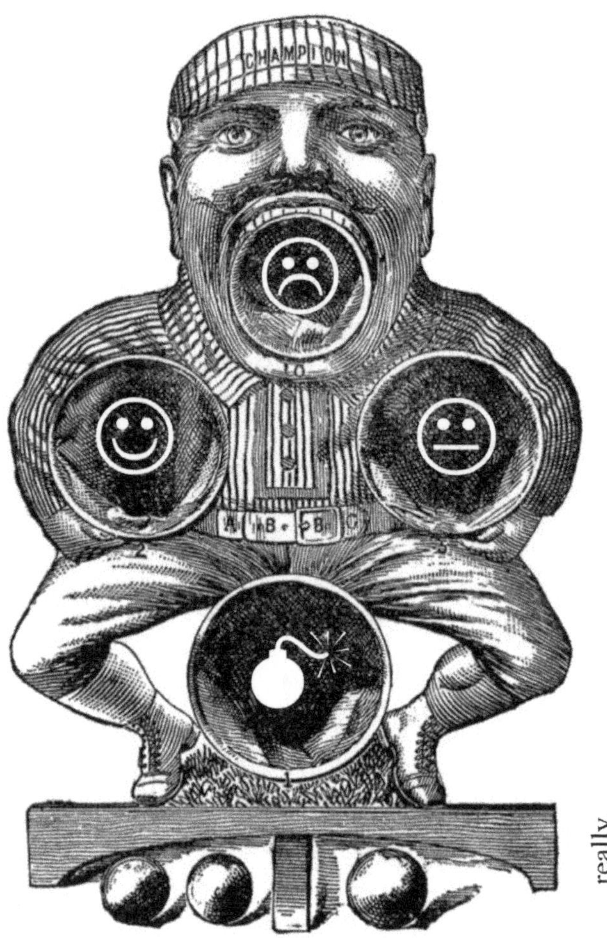

really.

and unchanged

Then someone said:

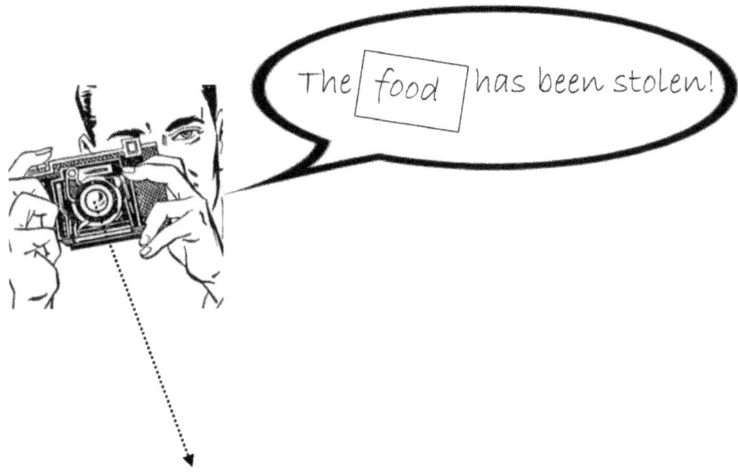

by a passing homeless person
who had put it in a red suitcase
in his shopping cart:

☒ after sweeping it off the table
☒ by the barbecue
☒ in the

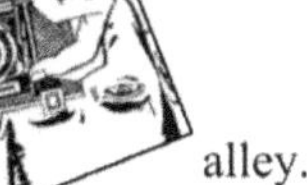

alley.

The fish was being done there

by the guy who always made the food

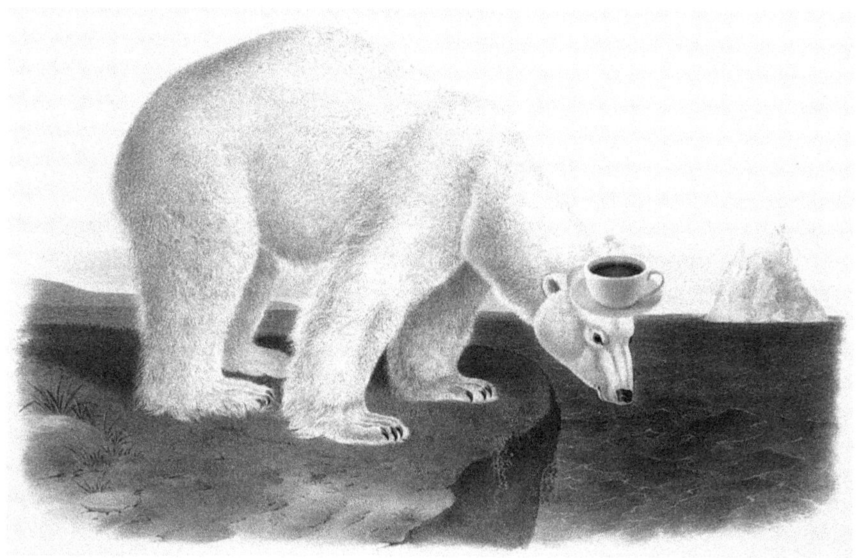

and had smelt very good

but there was more in the freezer

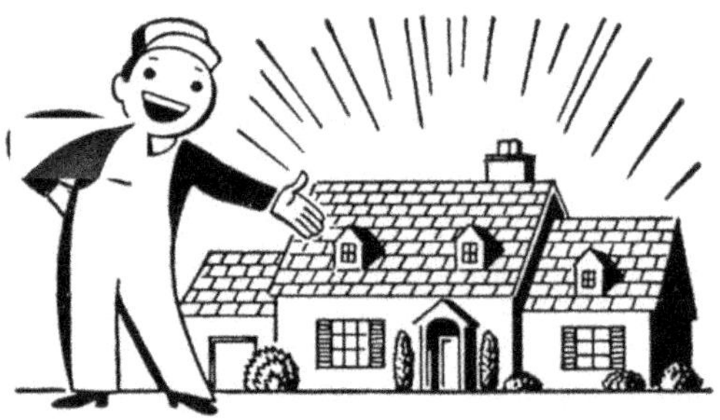

in the house.

The

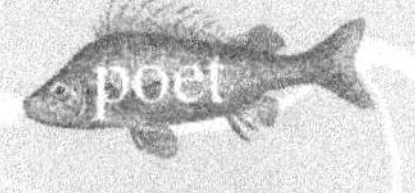

was indeed inside

In the living room!

said a man I remembered as an astute mind

who was now known as

Chatterbox

dressed

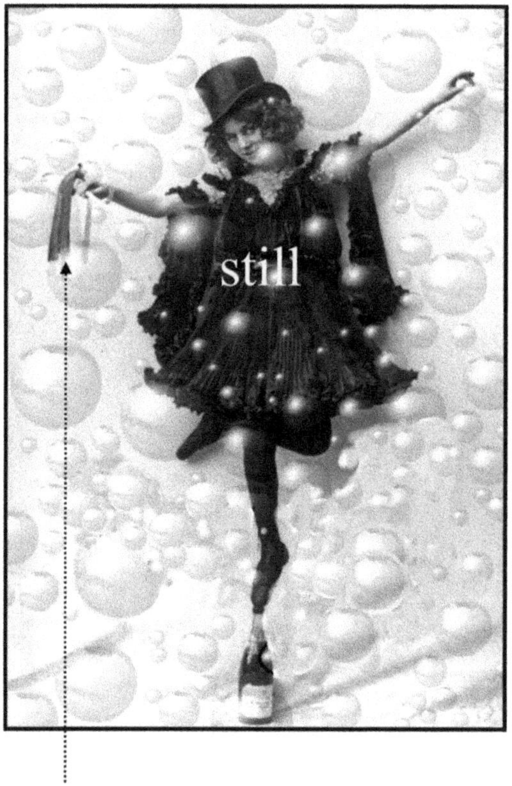

still

on this summer solstice day

in an Oxford wound scarf.

I heard the pioneer feminist next to him

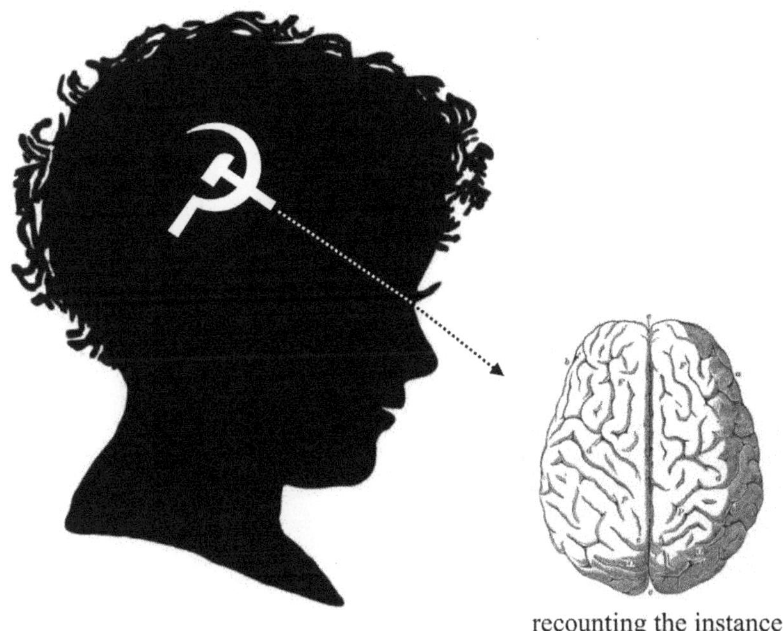

recounting the instance

at her **eldest** son's wedding

when her first husband,

she was his first wife of three,

asked her if she was ....→ related

to the bride.

I

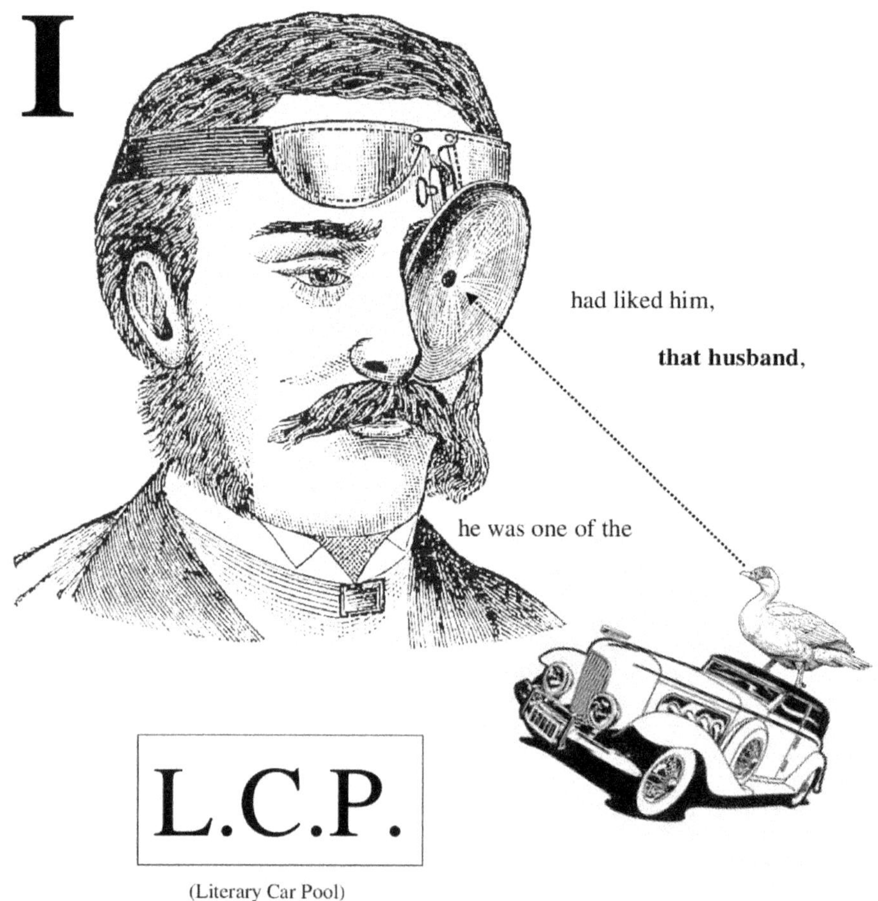

had liked him,

that husband,

he was one of the

L.C.P.

(Literary Car Pool)

which had gone from this house to the school
that had created this immortal movement

circled here around the wine table.

He was the only one who had asked:

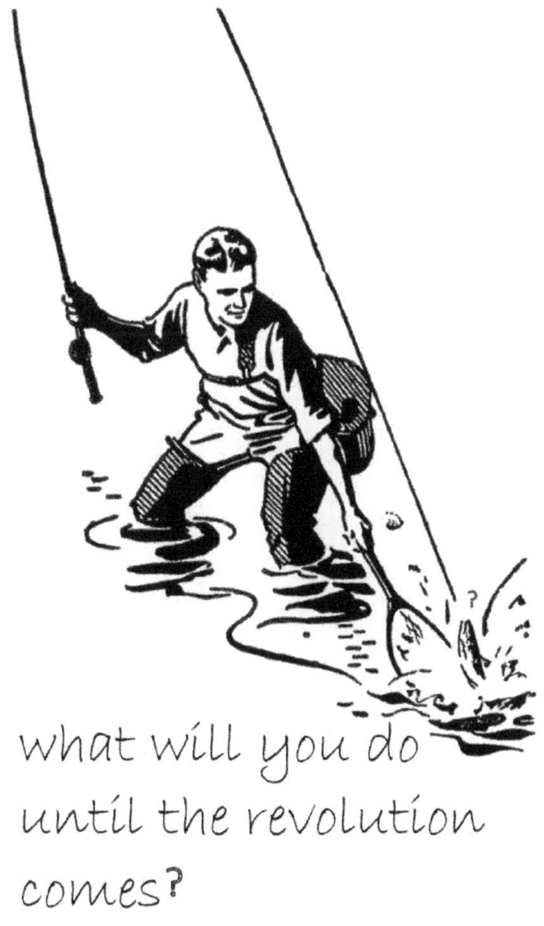

[?] The only one not a poet.

The poet was in black

with very little bling,

dressed

it was believed

by his last lover,

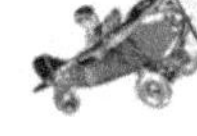

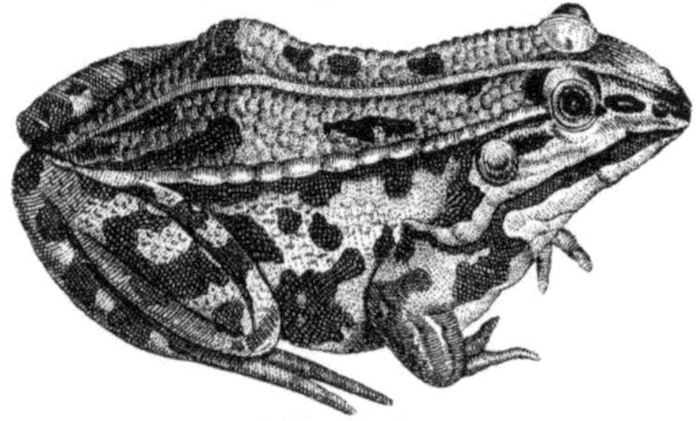

a person I knew to be very nice,

unlike *previous* lovers

who I now remembered had been exceptional

and historical.

Everything was falling into

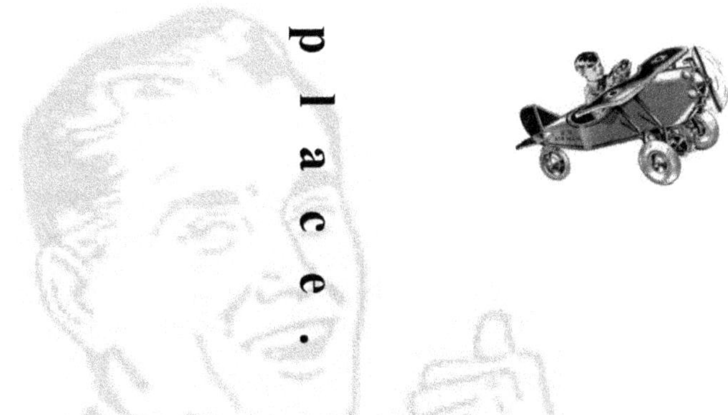

p

l

a

c

e

.

The hearse would soon arrive to take the poet

a

way.

There was no speculation voi¢ed here to follow on the literary or:

anyone's

position

in

industry

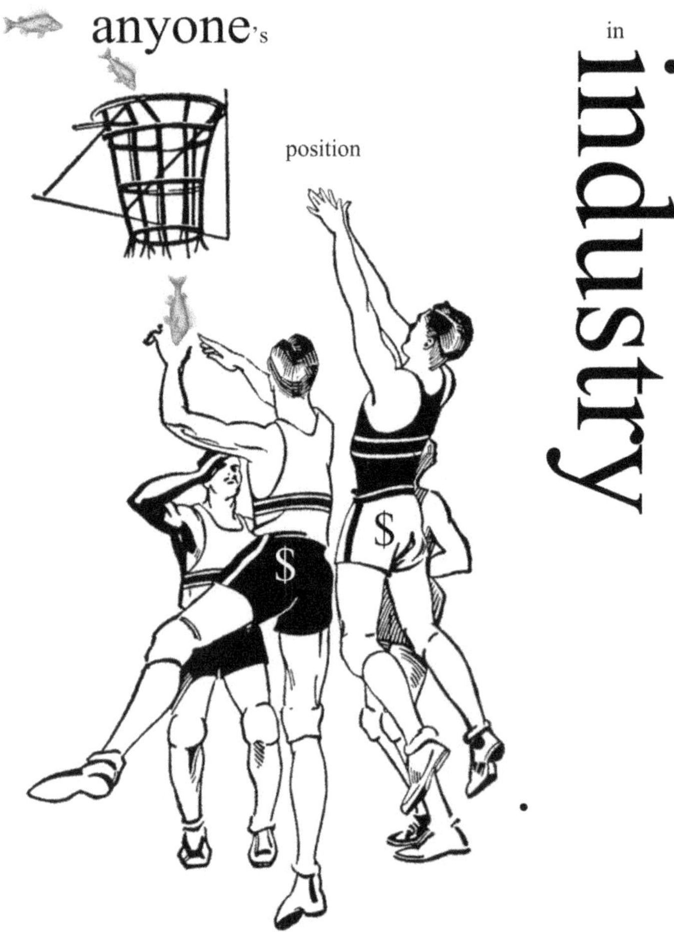

.

Only catching up on the very brief periods of time
the age grades had not seen each other
in this small town.

It was all:

☒ pleasant
☐ and neutral
as in sunshine and shade

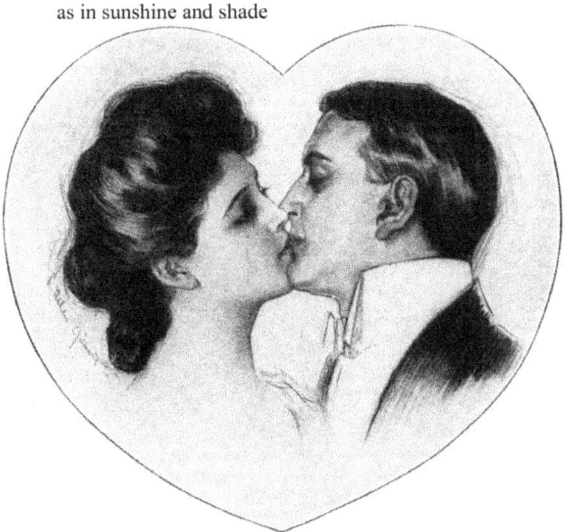

in the absence of both grace and bad manners.

There was some talk of persons absent.

It seemed warm.

But

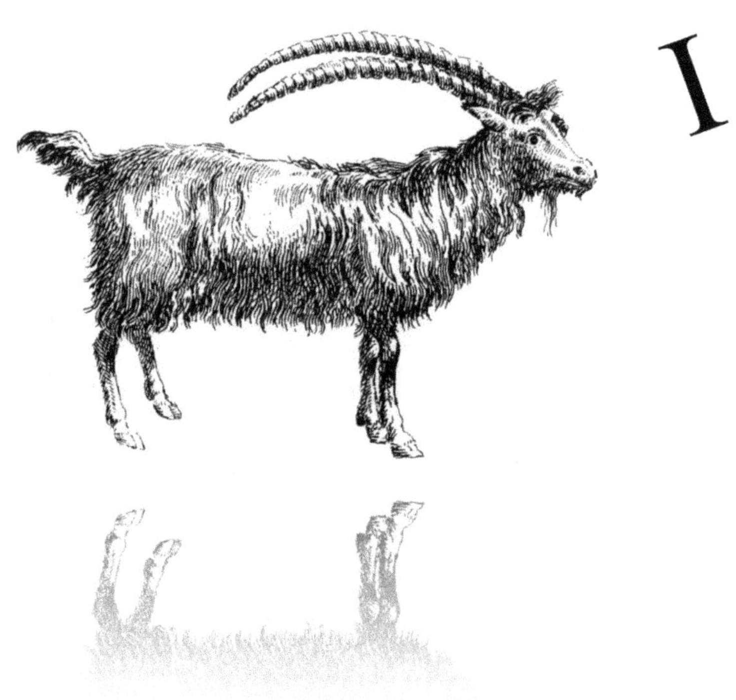

I

noticed

That:

seeming

☐ those who ~~were~~ the chorus of intellect
and life,
☐ of the new language
☐ spoke in the voices of large frogs

☒

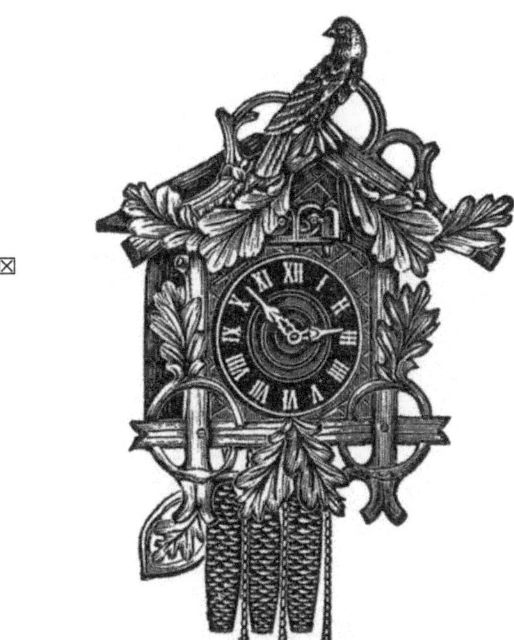

☐ and specks of darkness scattered across their

collective

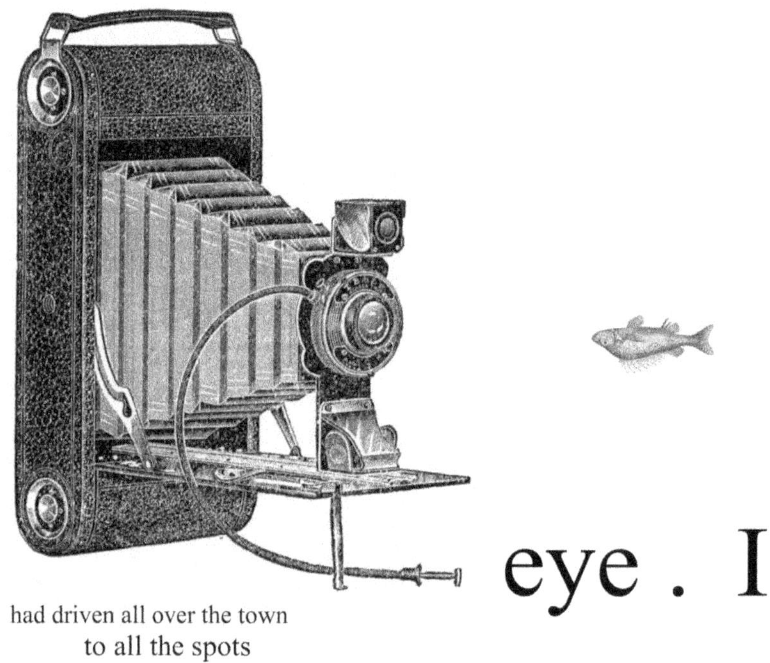

eye . I

had driven all over the town
to all the spots

before I found This
familiar and unchanged

p * l * a * c * e

just up from the water and down the hill.

As the hearse came up the alley,
and the wake attendees
whom I had seen as dung beetles
or alternatively scarabs

gathered around it,
I ran in my mind a weaving
of the conversations
I had had in the garden

and thought of

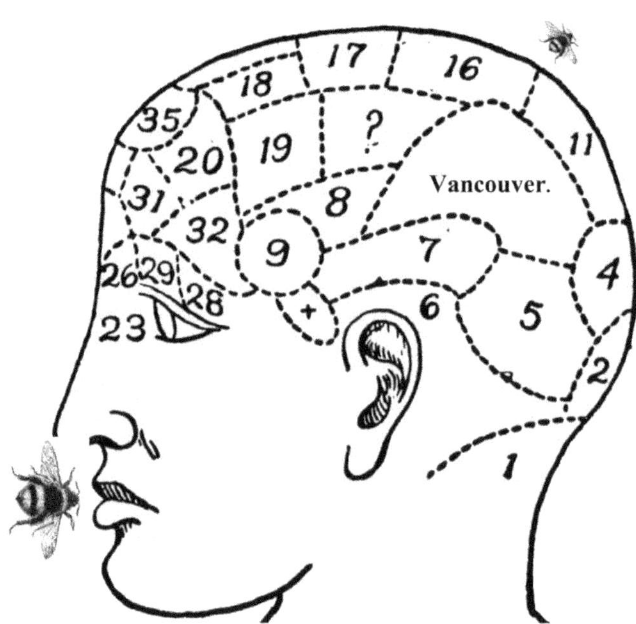

And this was entirely appropriate,

for the dead poet had reviewed my style
as:

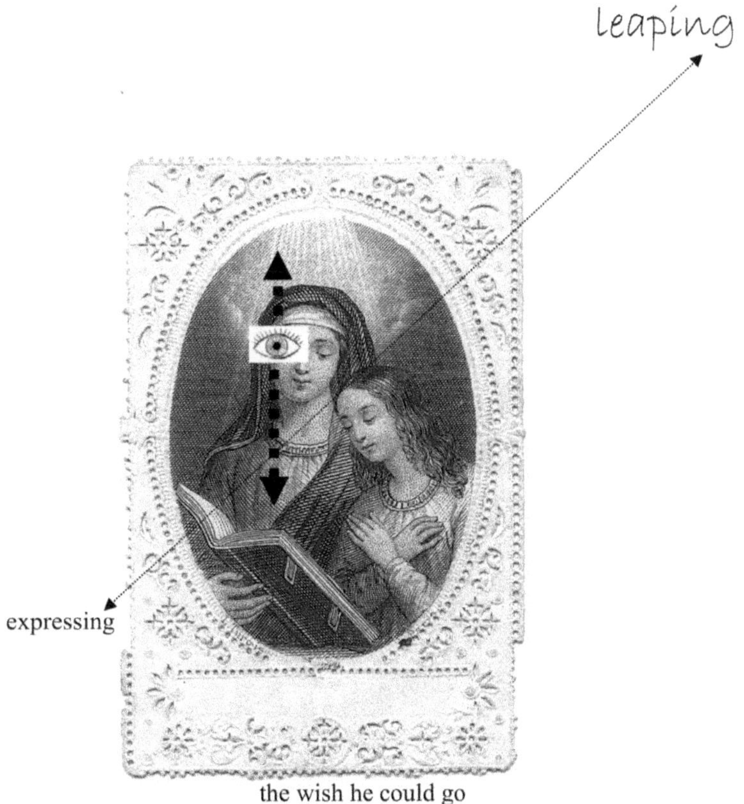

with everyone I invited

to the places I described.

I believe this was not just
only

his usual grace,

but:

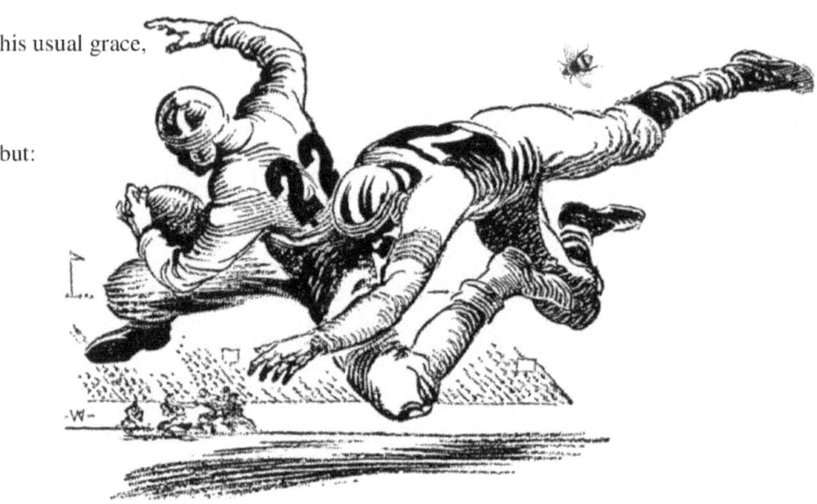

☒ actual sincerity,

because

he had also told me,
when I was inarticulate

although he didn't seem critical of that,

that he was

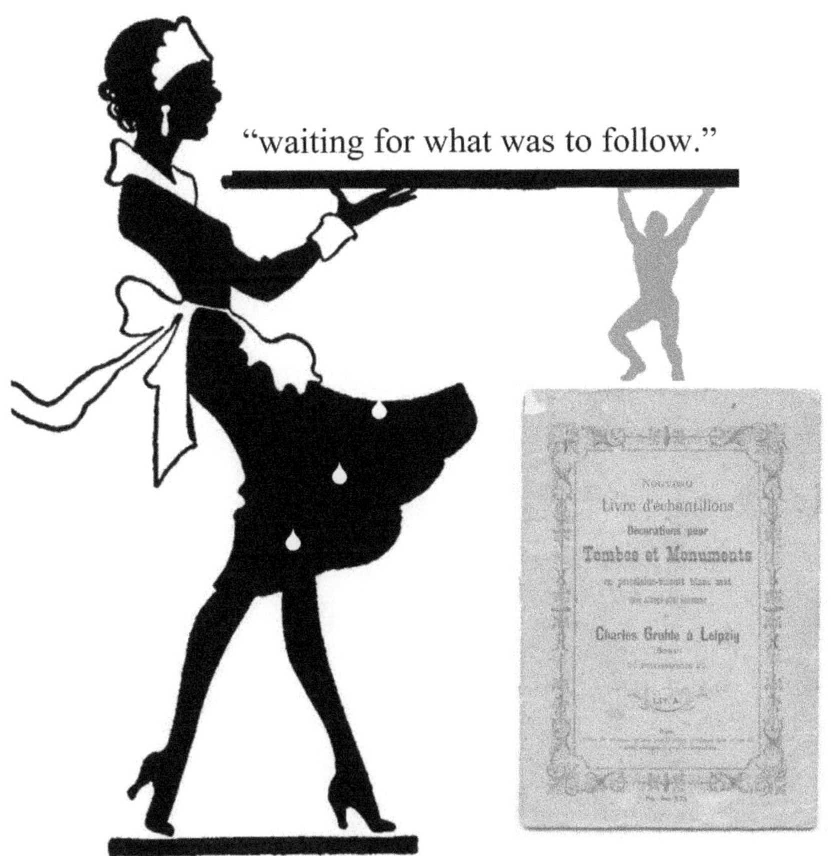
"waiting for what was to follow."
Livre d'échantillons
Décorations pour
Tombes et Monuments
Charles Gruhle à Leipzig

Also

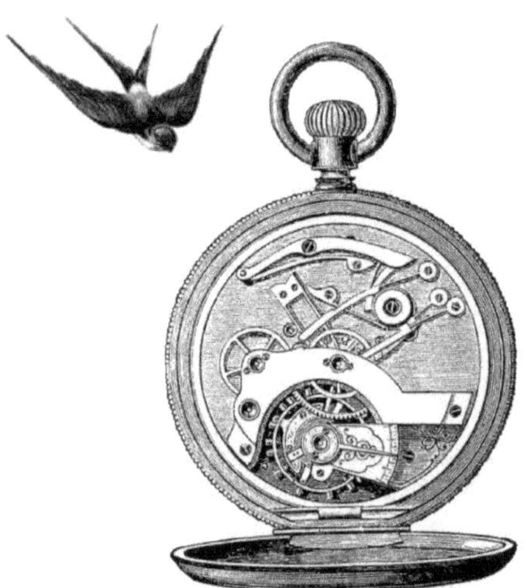

☒ the places I described were classical
☒ and literary
☒ and resplendent with association.

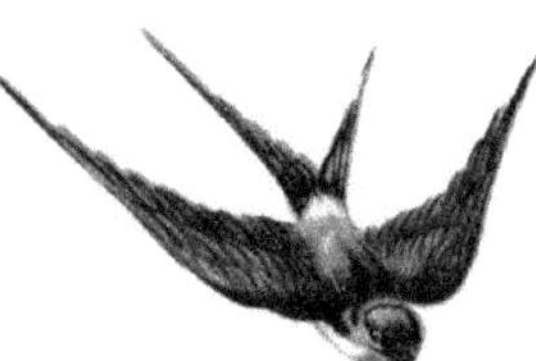

And, of course, I thought of the Vancouver
I had just driven through from the Fraser to False Creek.

Killing time.

Remembering

when I had driven it with a gun in the trunk
        or on the way

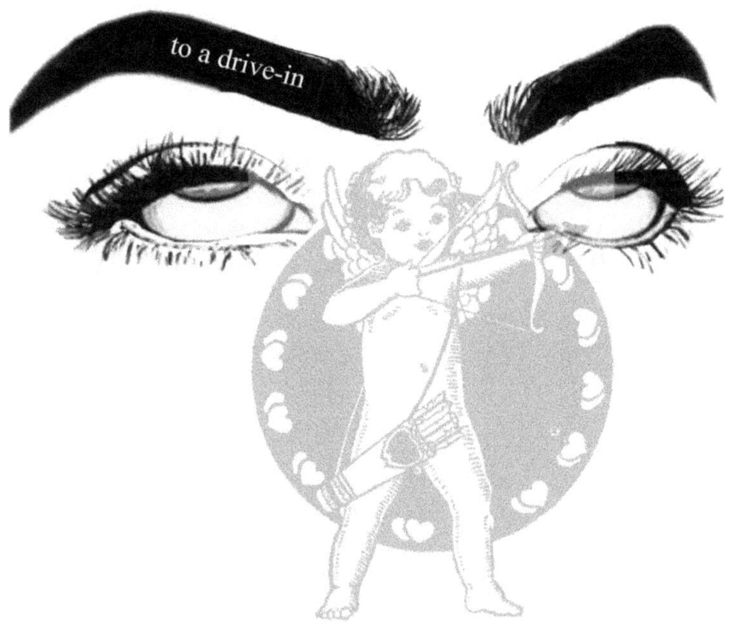

with a friend.

I had even gone into the

new-to me

hockey arena

after seeing a duck land on the empty parking lot

batting

the

air

as though it were the skipping dance
those ducks do.

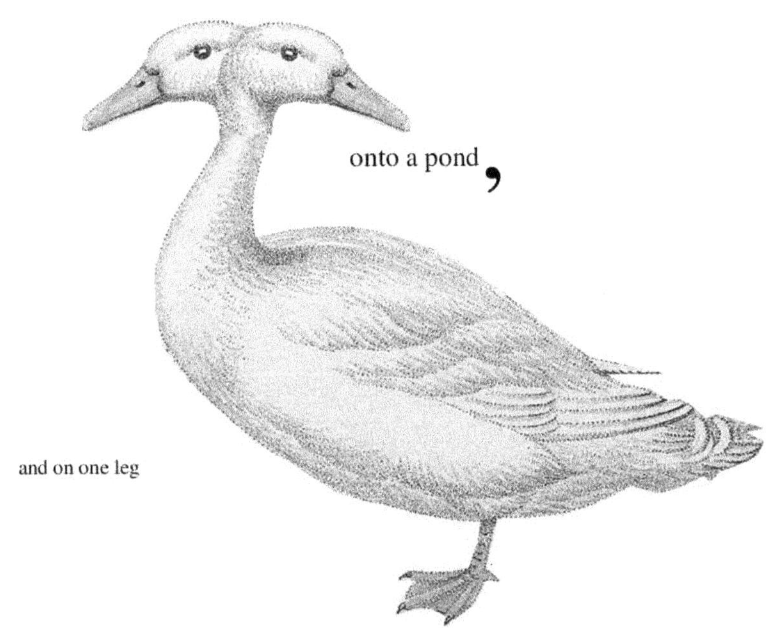

onto a pond,

and on one leg

then looking a r o u n d ,

quacking for friends.

'That is me'

,

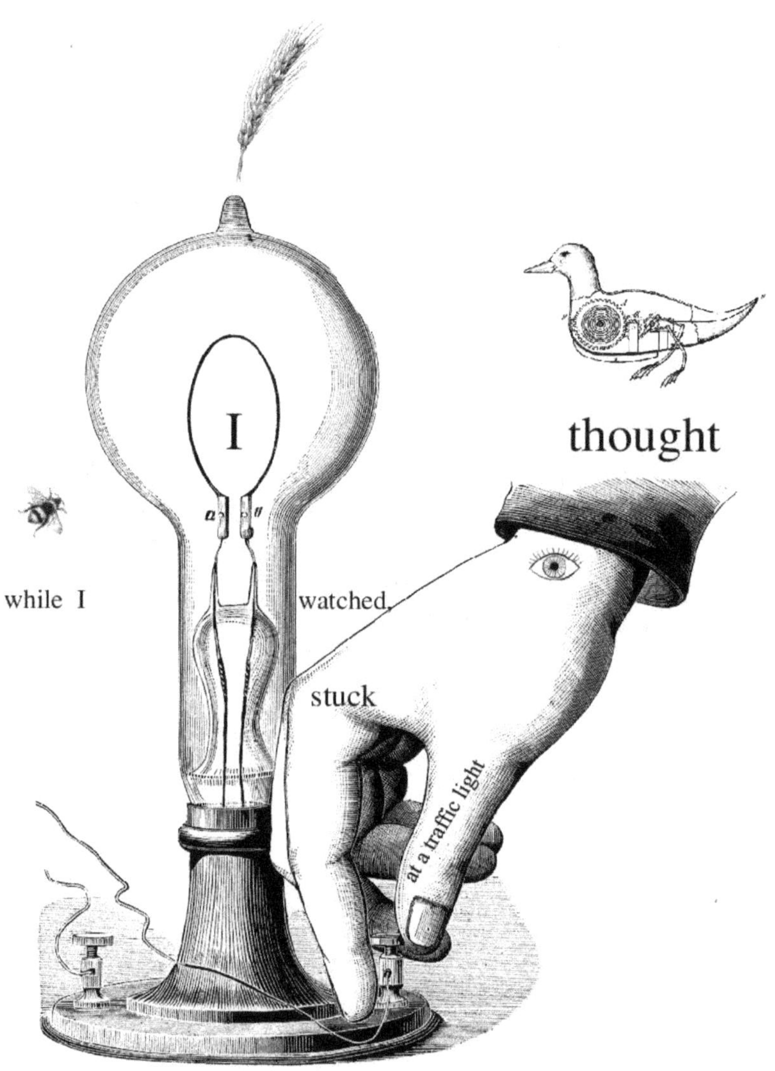
I
thought
while I
watched,
stuck
at a traffic light

I had turned into the lot to see
what else the duck would do

but:

I T

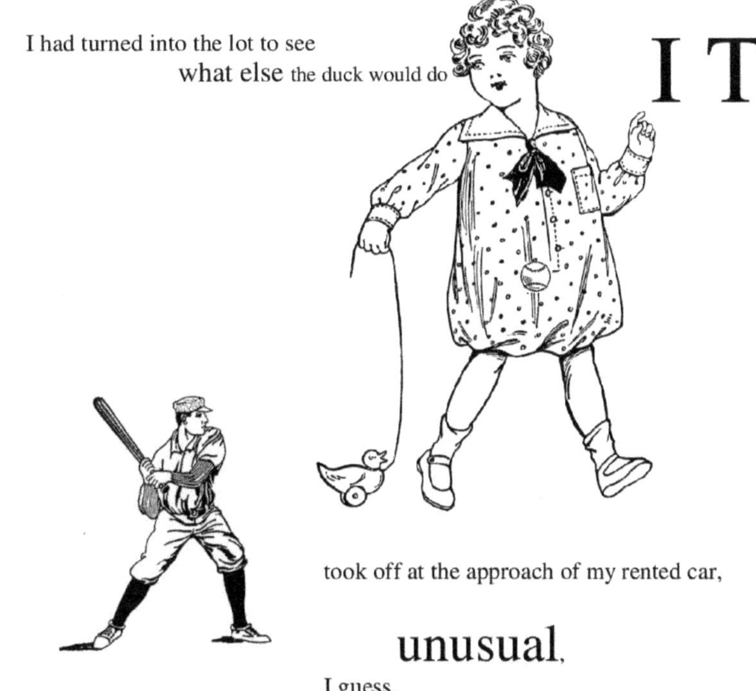

took off at the approach of my rented car,

unusual,

I guess,

for the season and time of day,
so then I decided:

'let's see

if the stadium is empty.
It isn't the coliseum

for heaven's sake'.

And it was.

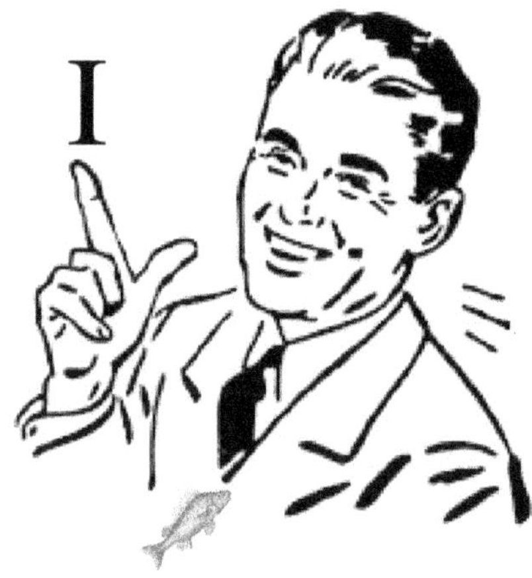

went in.

And:

there in the foyer was the

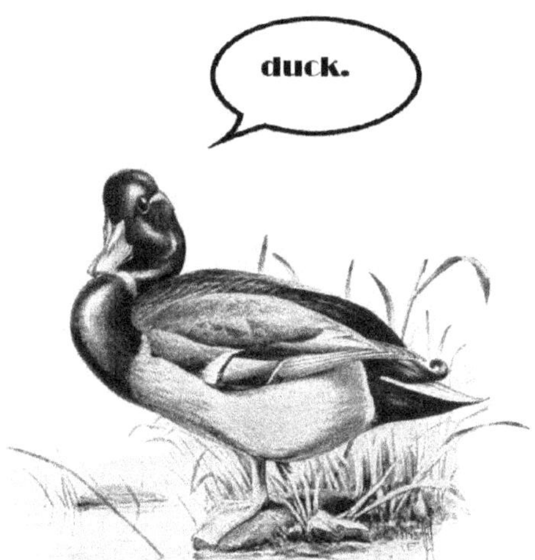

it seemed as though

it wanted to say s*o*m*e*t*h*i*n*g

so then I left.
I wasn't going to start

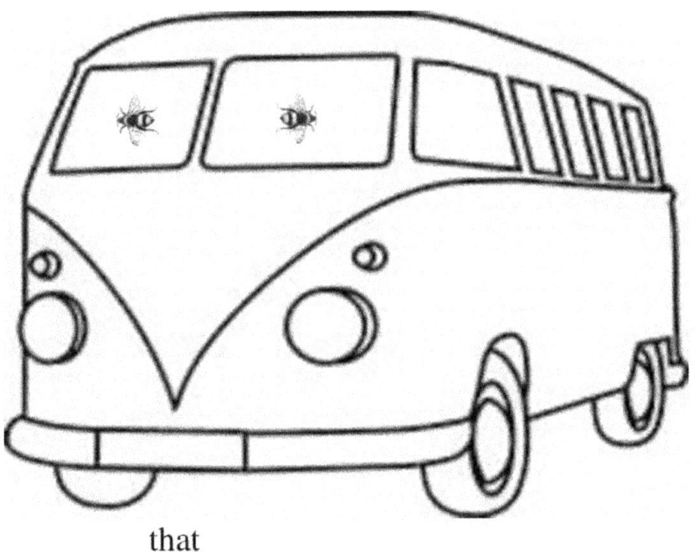

that

again.

This musing on the hearse's

arrival

began with a brief passage of mental leaping

about Gwen Pharis Ringwood,

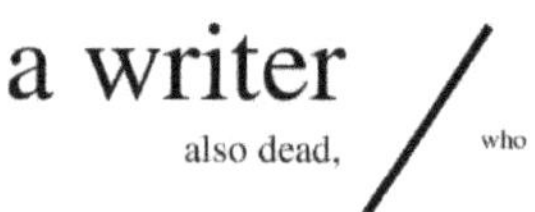

is obituarized in many voluminous
Companions to Liter~~choor~~ature

with regret

as having left the Canadian mainstream

of writing

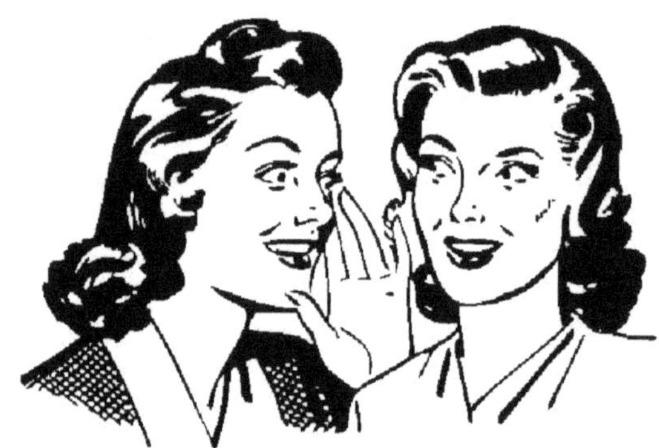

after "she moved to…"

"William's Lake."

There is a theatre
named after her

in William's Lake.

There is ~~no-one~~ *none* in

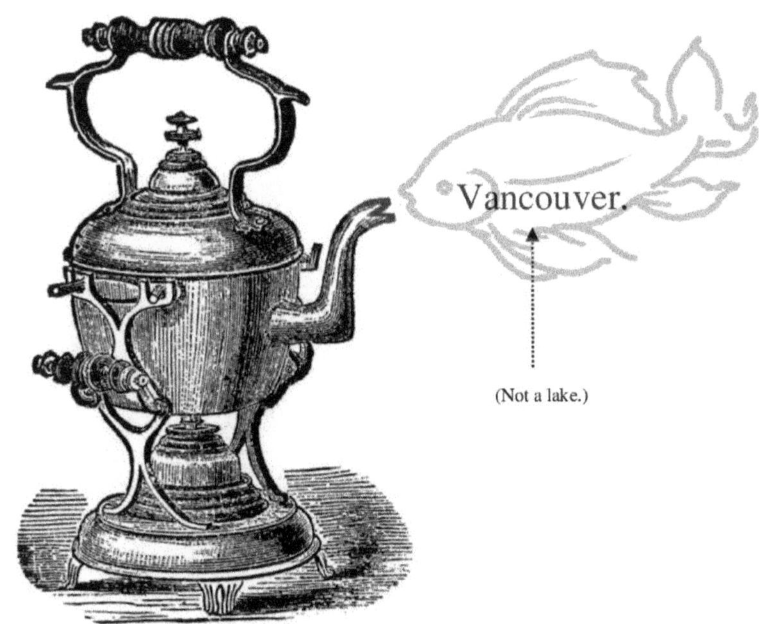

I wondered about a beach
or at least a Japanese Cherry tree

~~about~~ after

the dead

to go

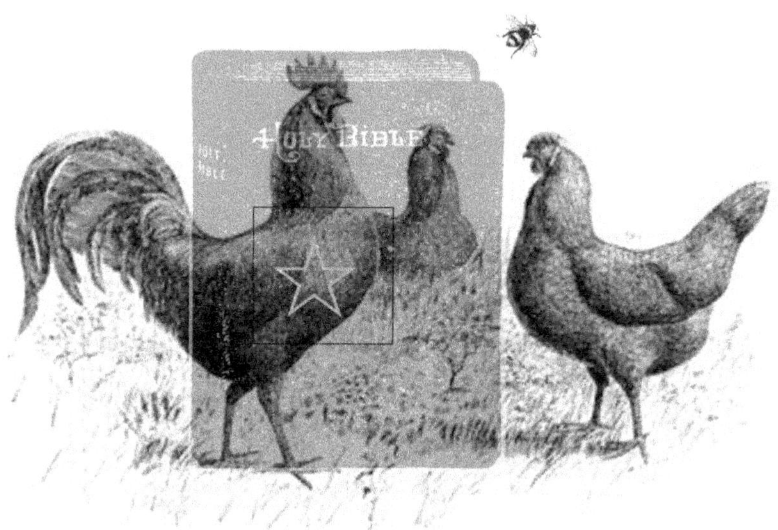

with the inevitable industry of critical books
by the schools of successors.

Then I began a mental comparison of the crack houses
of the so-called

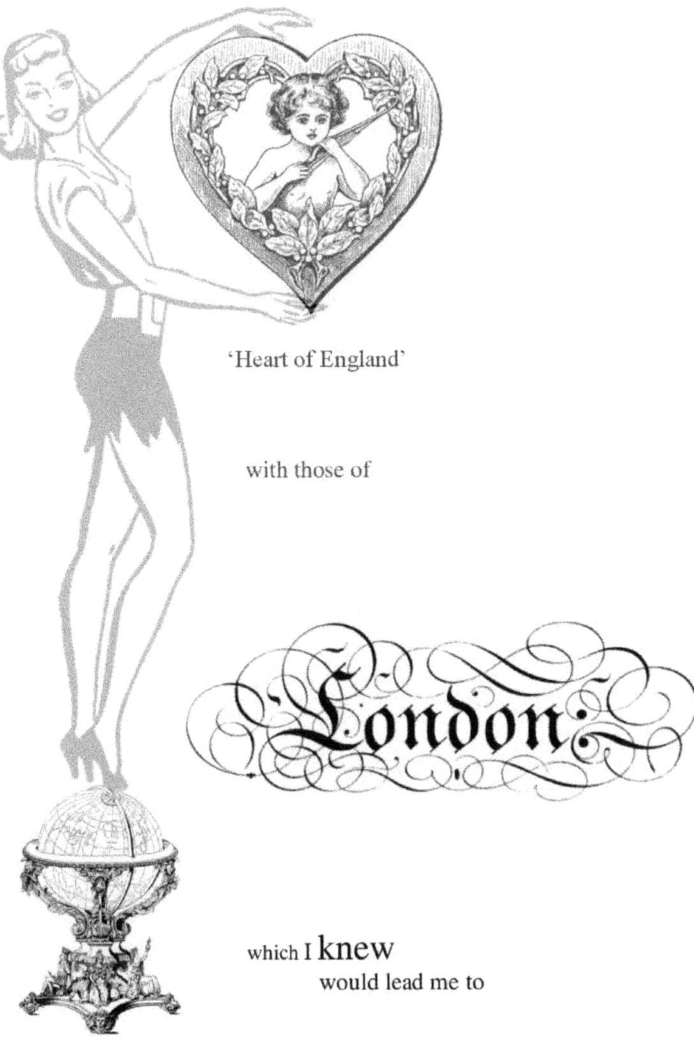

'Heart of England'

with those of

which I knew
would lead me to

"thinking about"

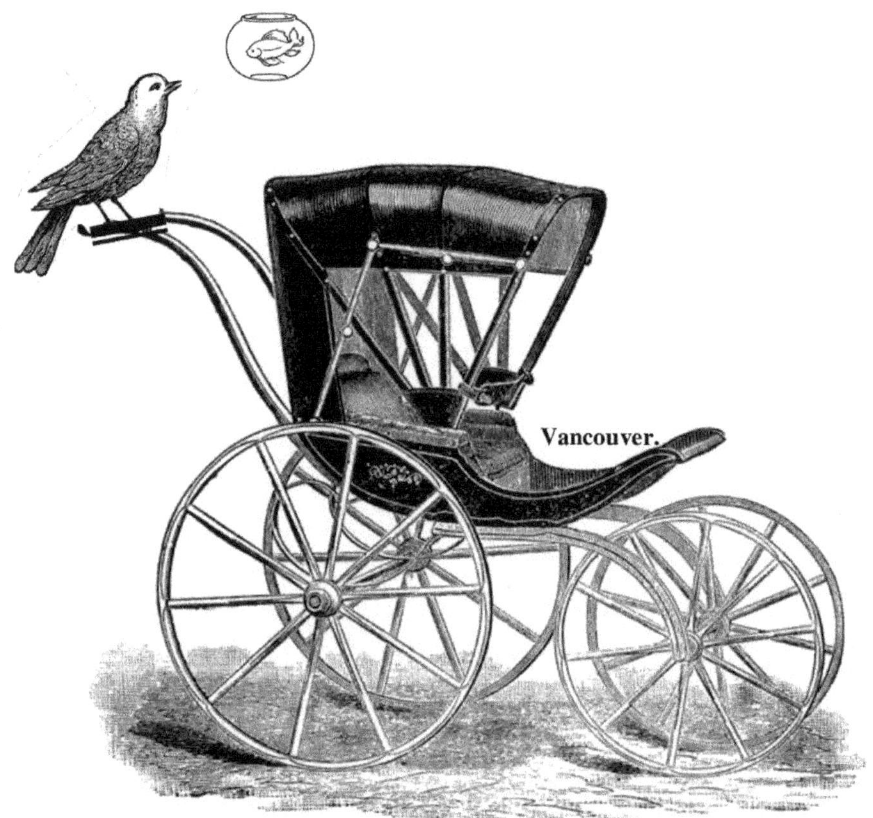
Vancouver.

The crack houses of Middle England

tend to be in estates
backing onto rural

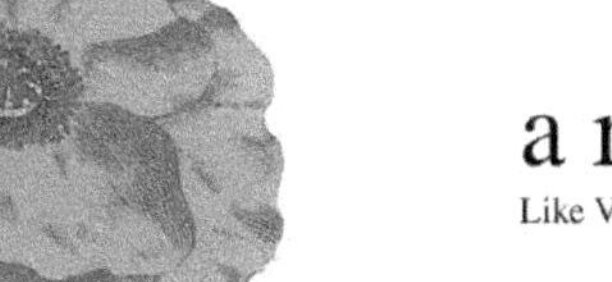

a r e a s.
Like Vancouver.

They usually have

g a r d e n s

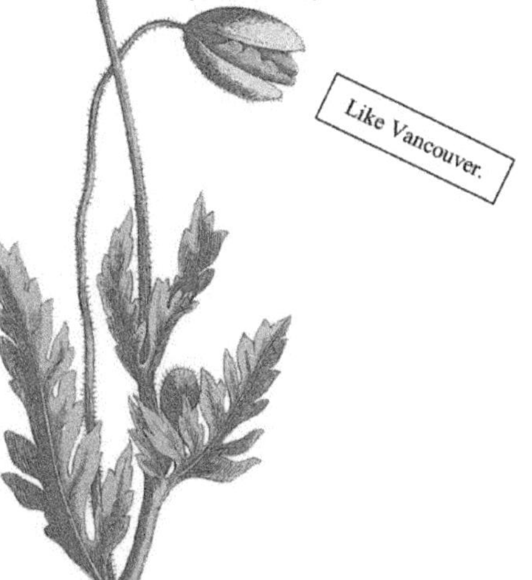

which,

although encrusted with dog shit
often
and the odd hulk of a car
still have some

space.
Like

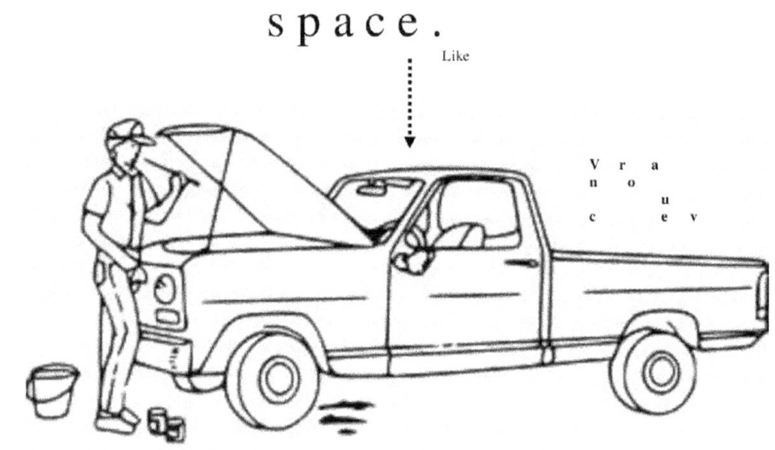

The child abusers and Satanists of

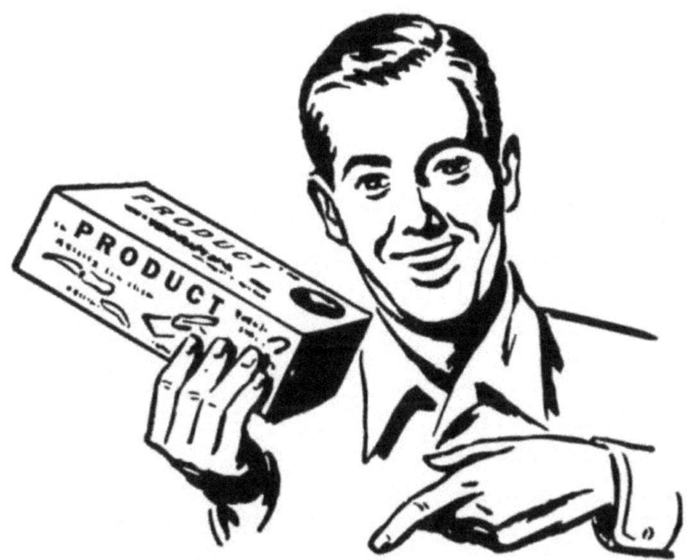

Middle England

usually fantasize with easily identifiable cartoon references

to:

☐ act out
☒ comic books and
☒ popular images from

at times

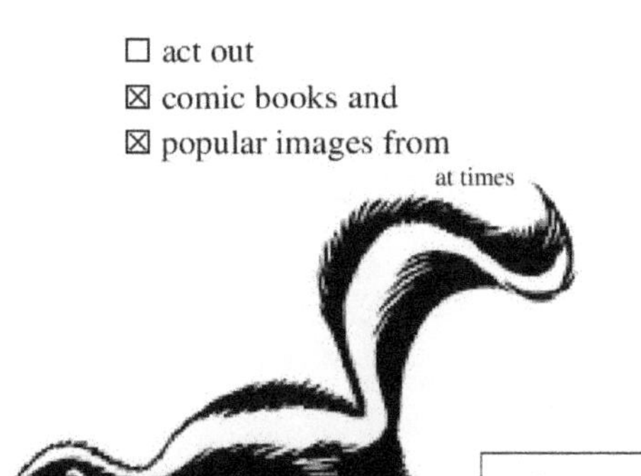

airport novels.

Assessments of the crack house

habitués

of England

resemble those of

the testimonies of

child abusers.

They see their activities as lifestyle

choices.

The gardens are not like

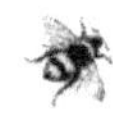

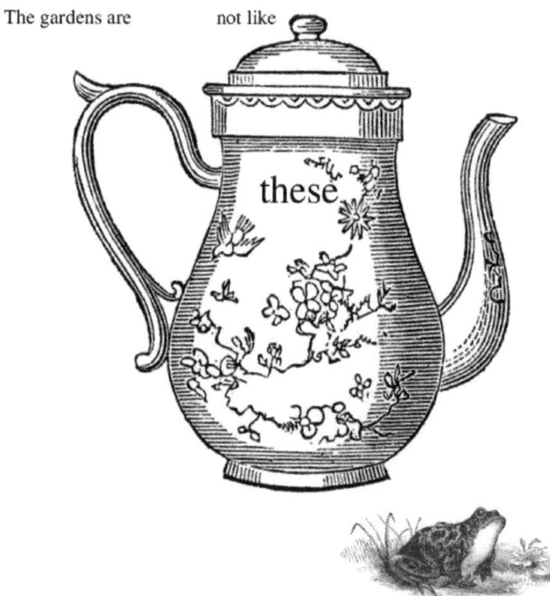

these

The crack houses of London

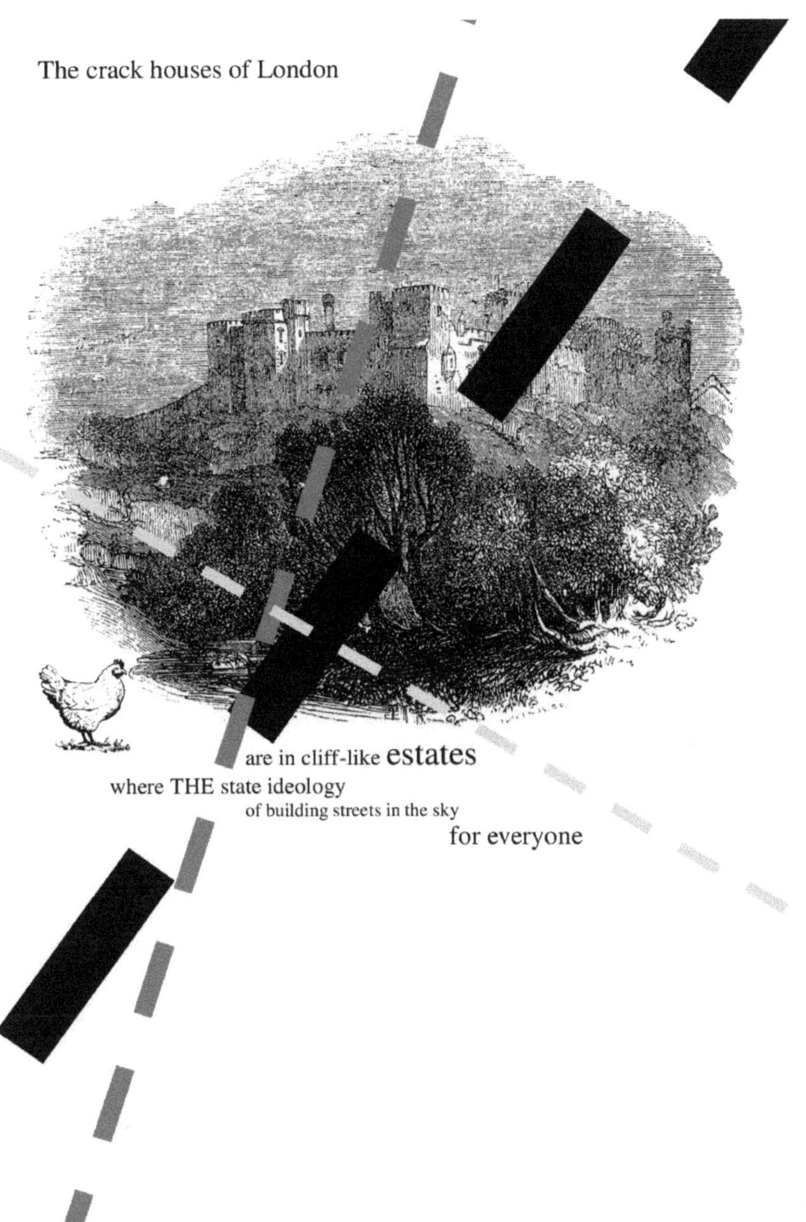

are in cliff-like estates
where THE state ideology
of building streets in the sky
for everyone

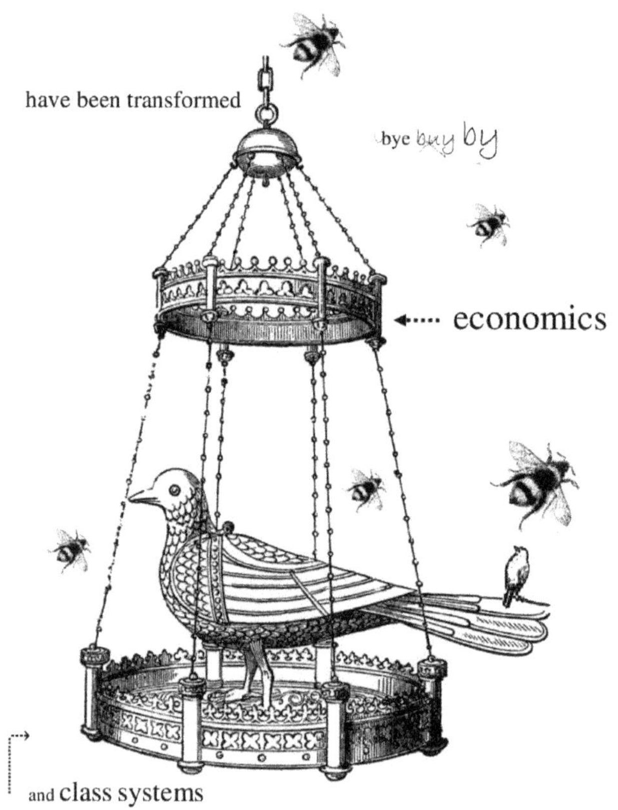

into small nations of lumpen proletariat

where state power
does NAUGHT Knot

not

go.

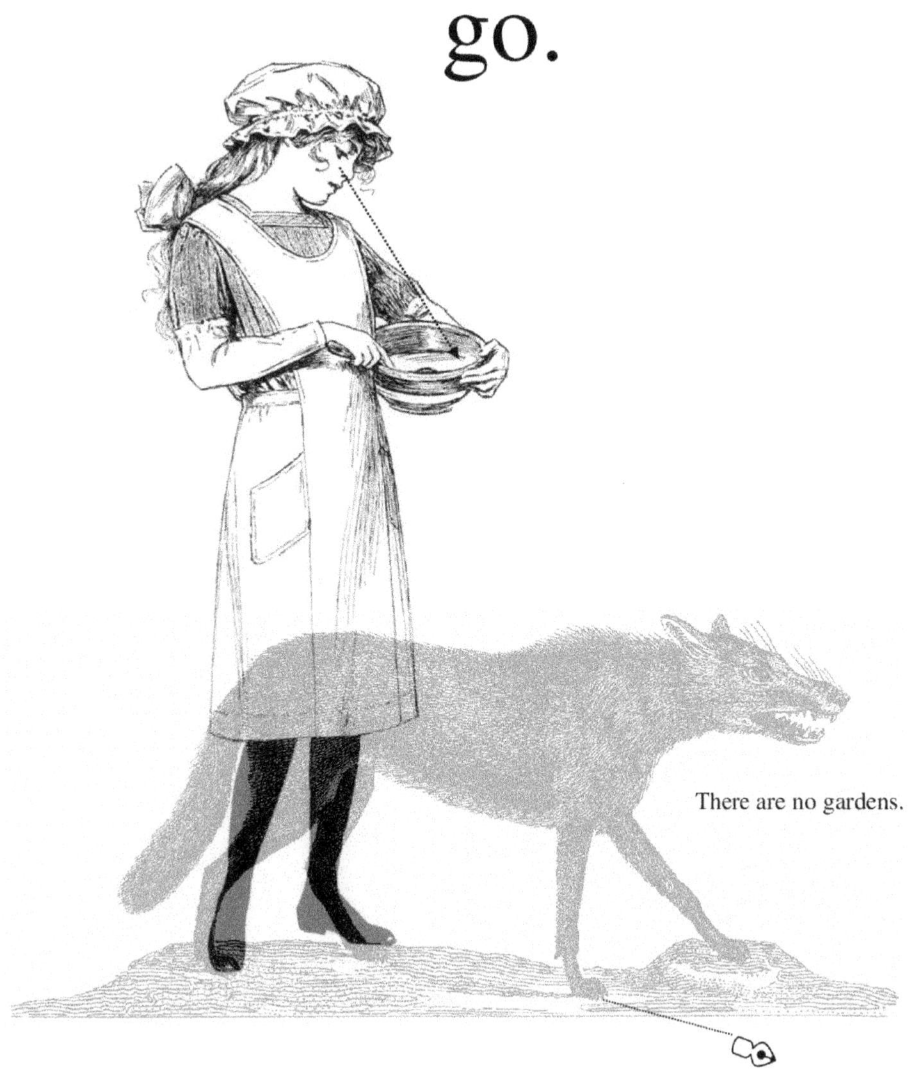

There are no gardens.

The child abusers

of several genders and national

orIgIns

there

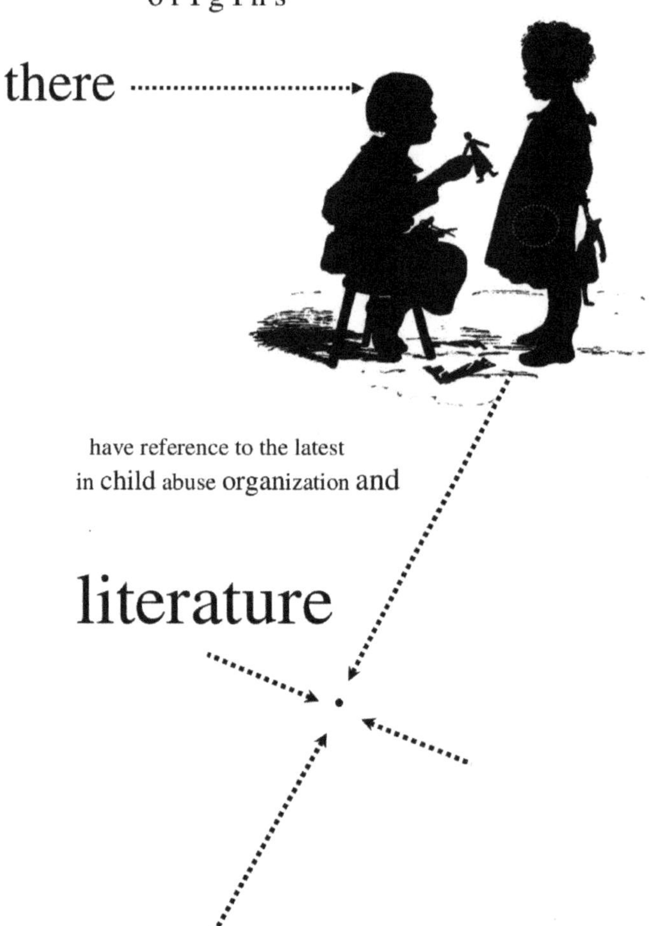

have reference to the latest

in child abuse organization and

literature

They are determined in

assert~ing~

themselves
and finding

~~there~~ their

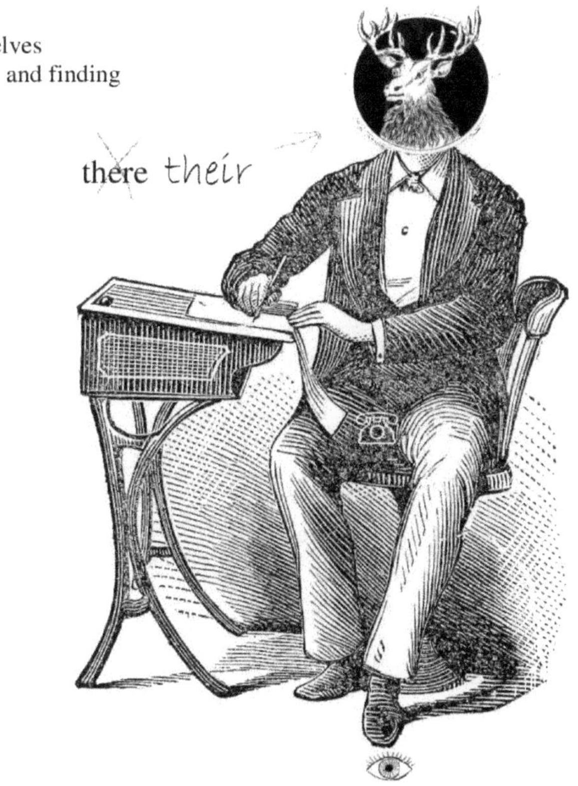

DES~TINY~.

They are largely
believed to be incurable
and so

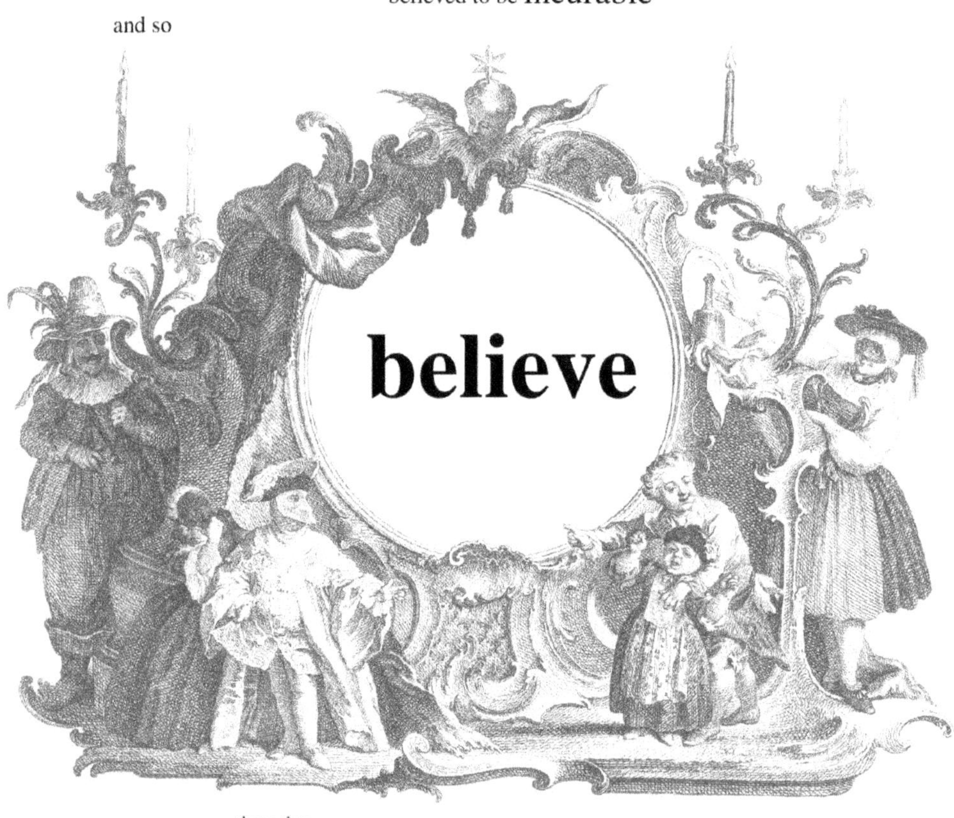

believe

themselves.

They are intimate with police science and forensics
from research on the web.

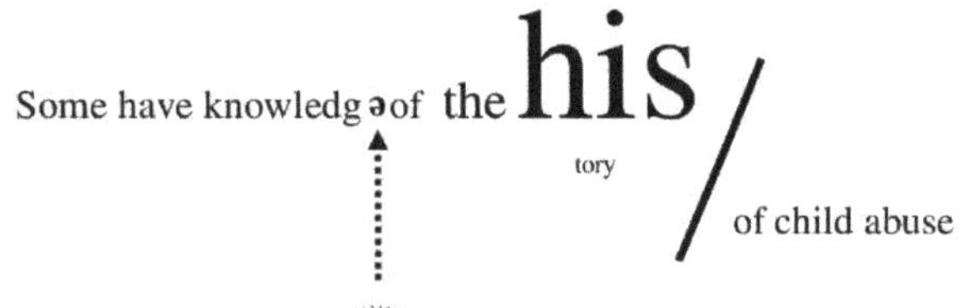
Some have knowledgəof the his
tory
of child abuse

literature.

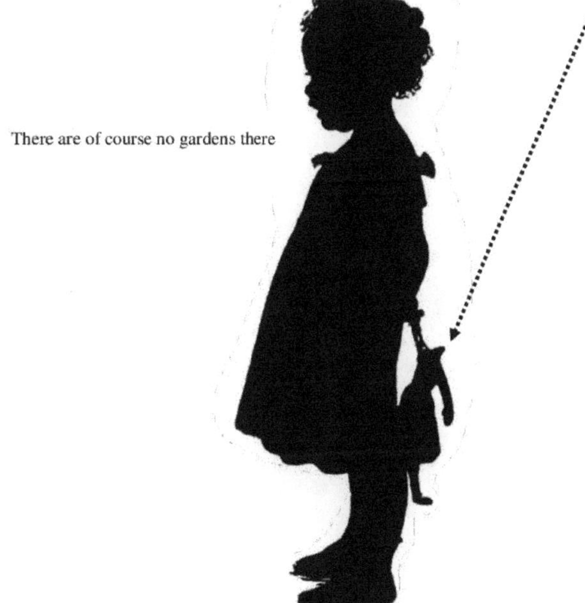
There are of course no gardens there

But corpses are sometimes found in the dust bins

by walkways,

It is a pedestrian society

connected to cruising expensive cars

and aspirational motorcycles

by

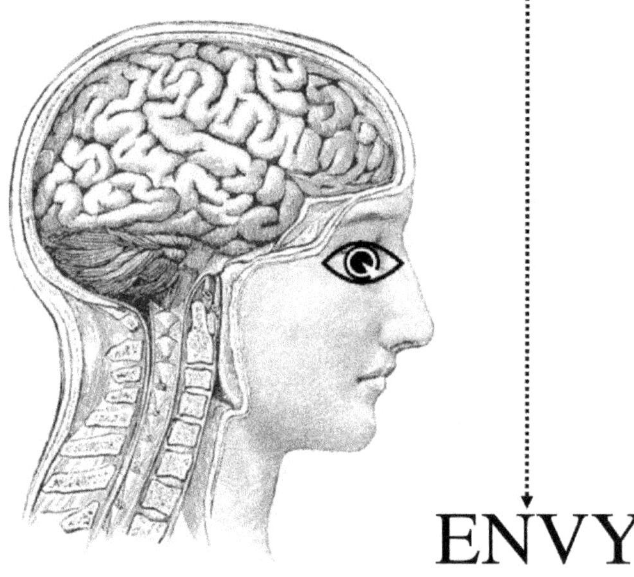

ENVY

of the lower

echelons,

the counts and countesses of each floor,

who report to the **Dukes**

of the estate buildings

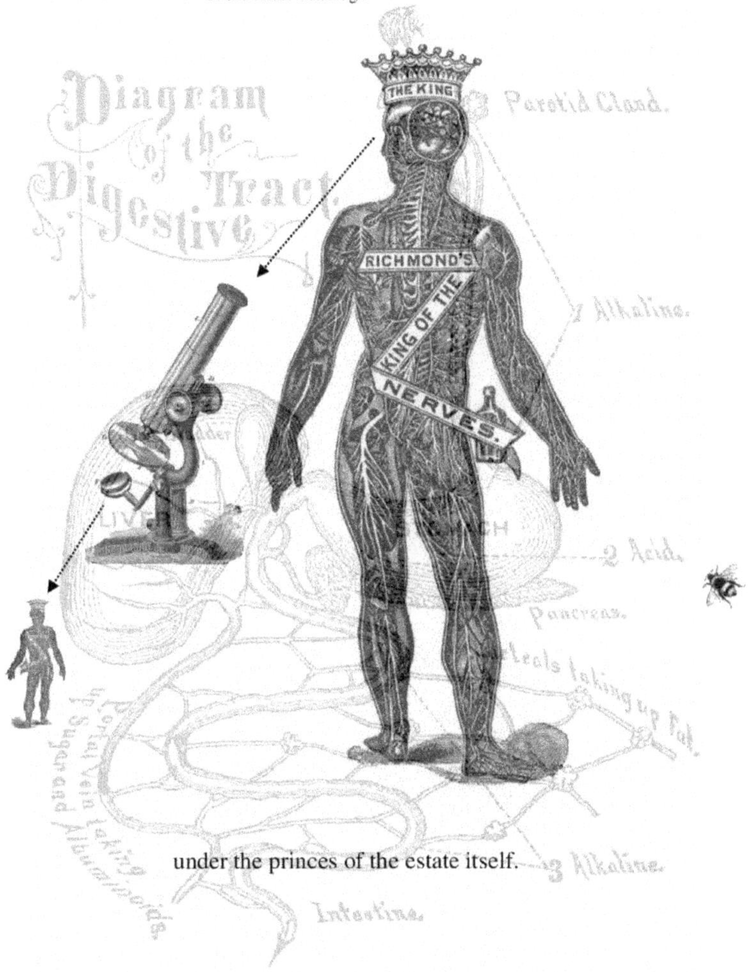

under the princes of the estate itself.

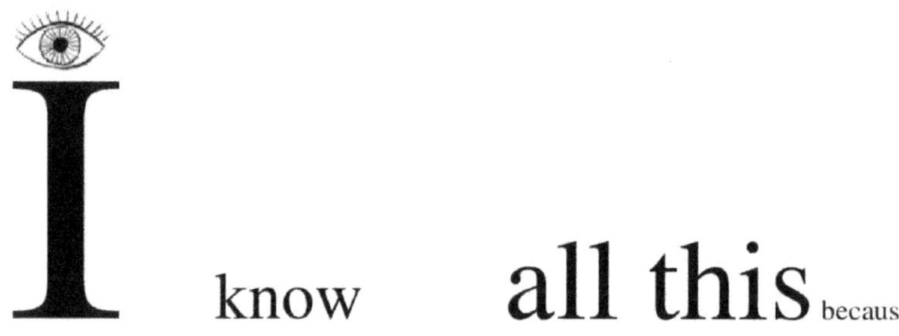

I know all this because

I have been involved with investigating cases
on these estates

and have studied mediaeval social structure

which is not as one thinks from reading popular

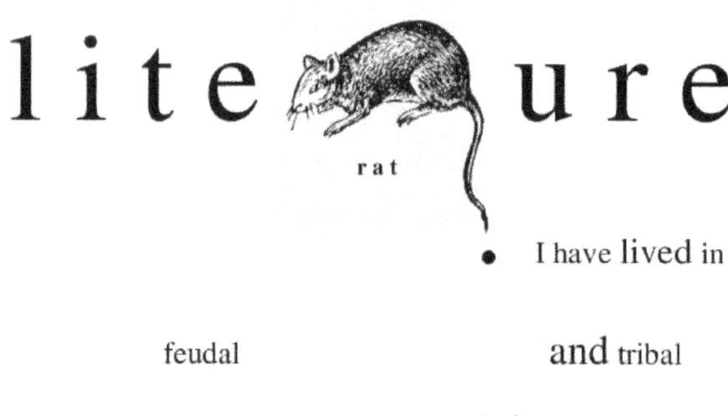

lite rat ure

I have lived in

feudal and tribal

societies.

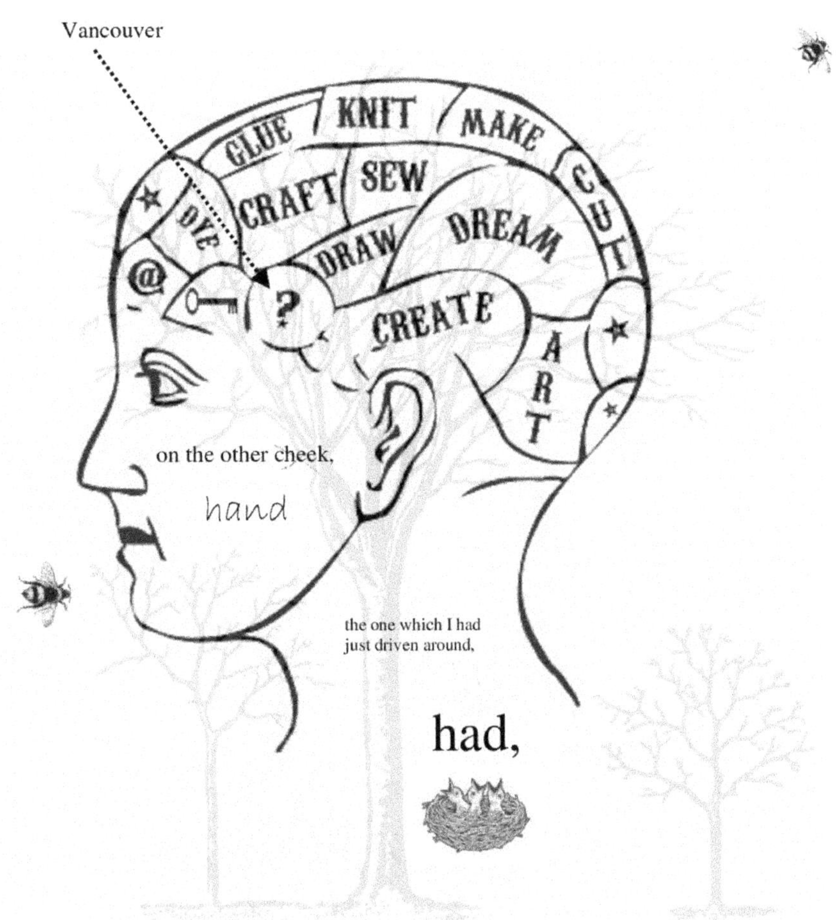

except for three-thronged streets,

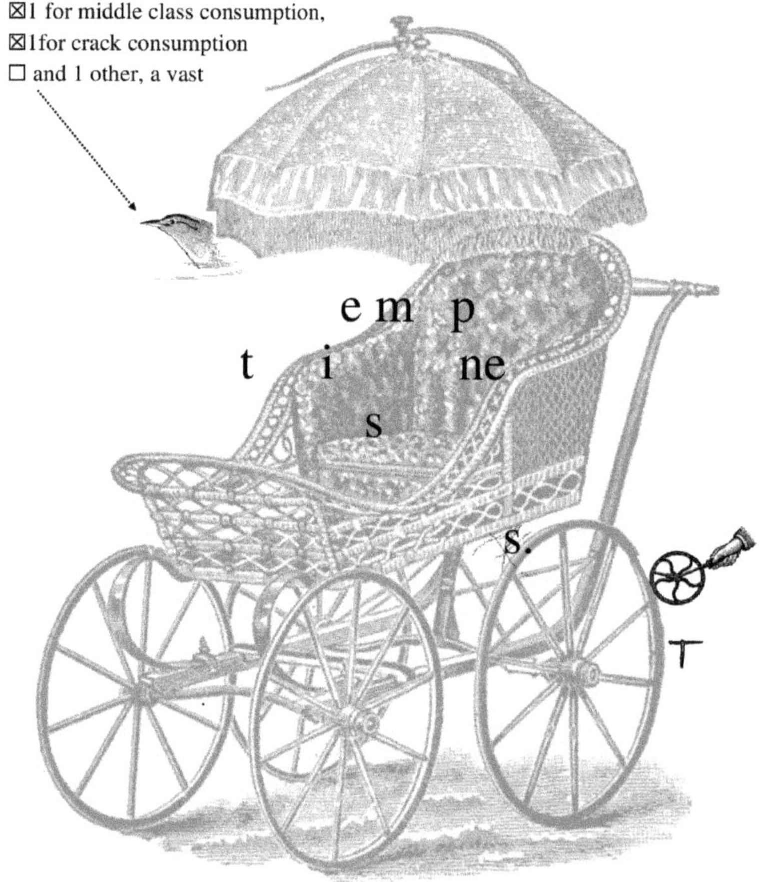

A barren land

which seems full

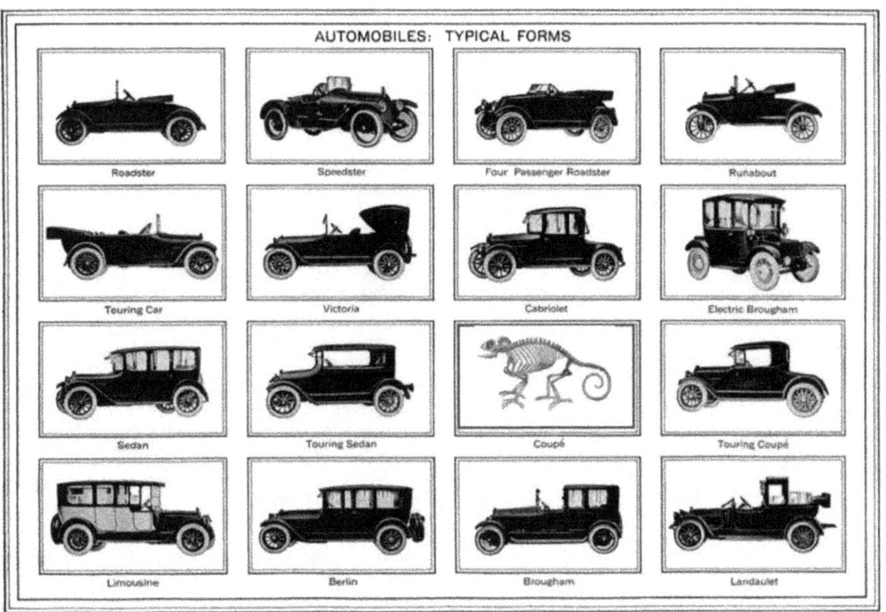

because of the cars.

The people on the full streets walk symbolically.

There is,

for example:

☒ the stiff legged heel first walk,
hands clasped behind back

☐ or folded over chest
by gender

☒ to indicate thoughtful judgement

of consumable items

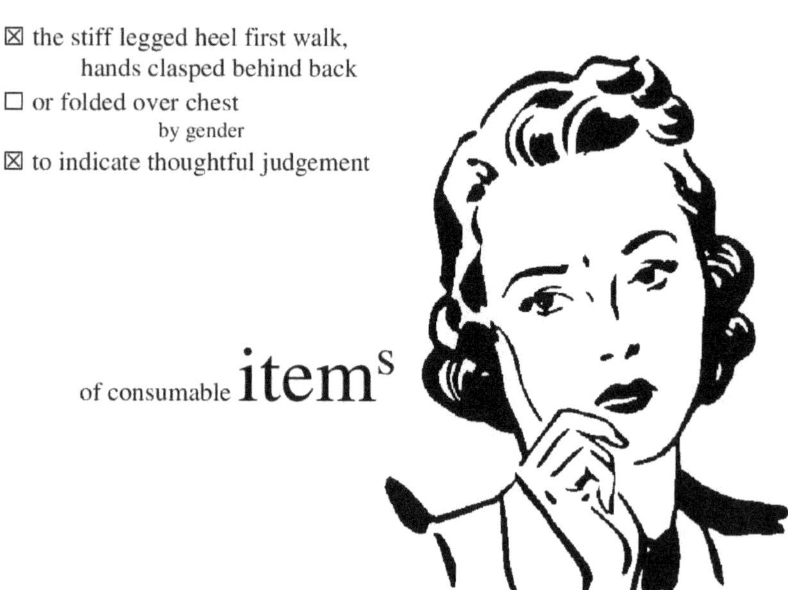

including the gifts of nature.

The female groupings

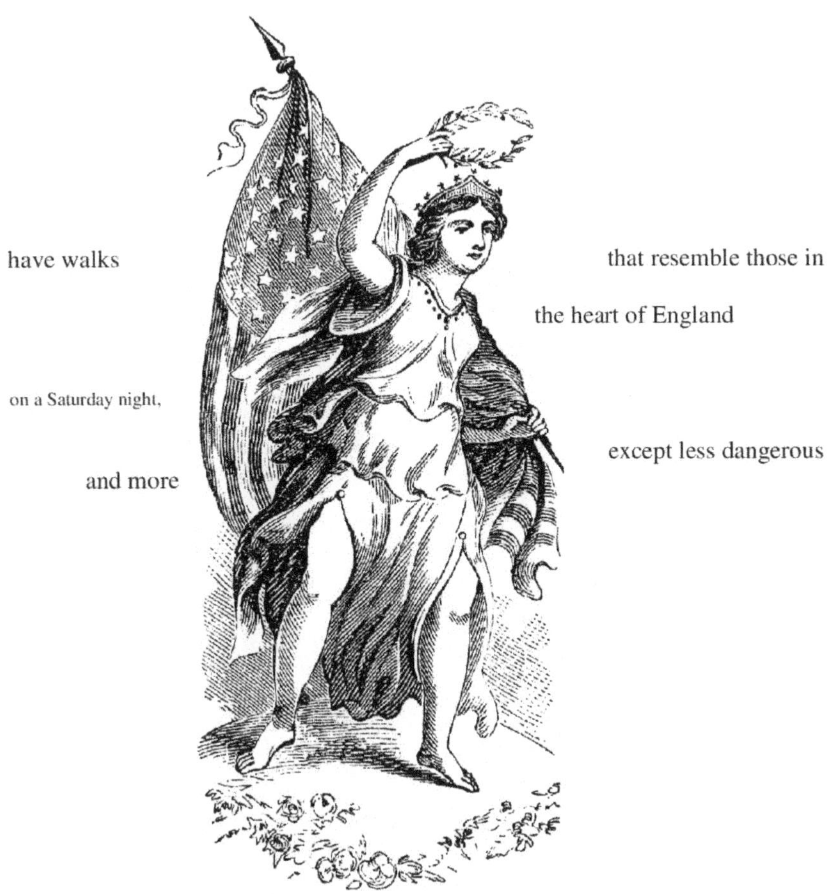

have walks

that resemble those in

the heart of England

on a Saturday night,

except less dangerous

and more

theatrical

You

have the bouncy eyes focused on the point
ahead in time and place,

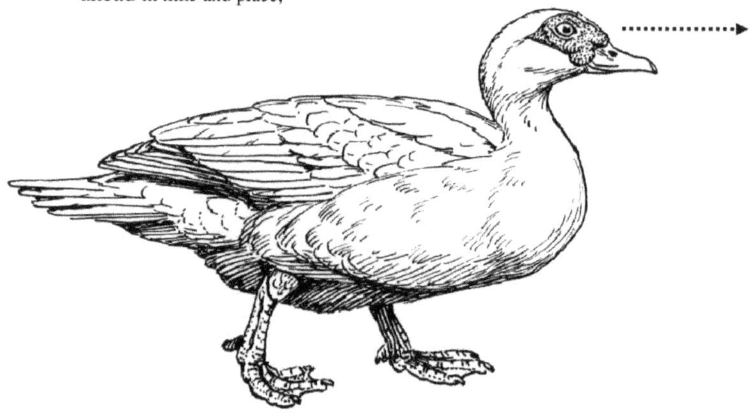

walk d e l i b e r a t e l y,
striding to the important event
with the

'what are **YOU** looking at'

stiffness

belying any risk taken in:

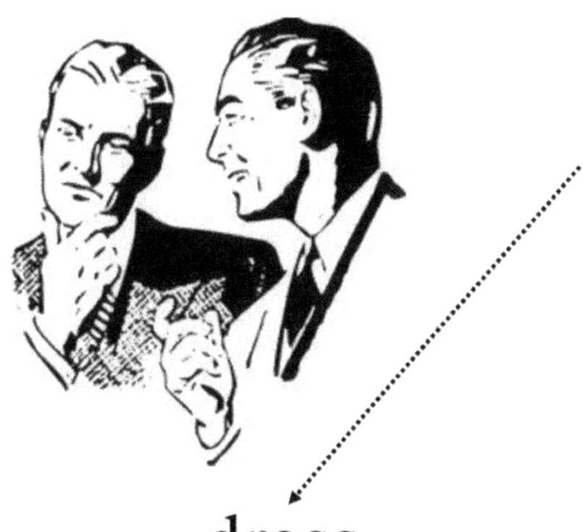

drəss.

and also the loping,
bouncing,
groupings of

movie ~~jingle~~ jungle

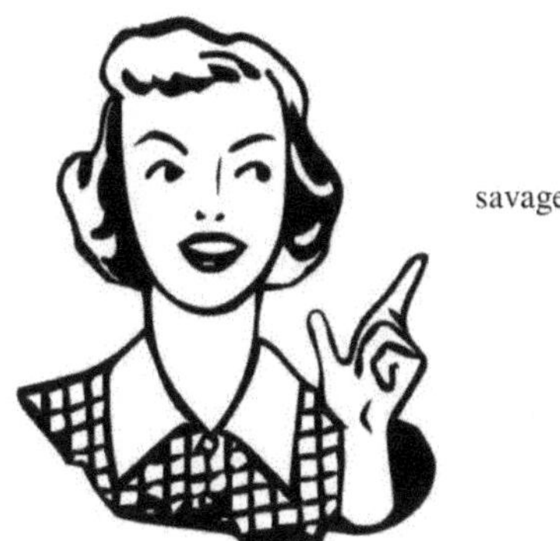

savages,

uniformed in the exact gradations and colour schemes of fashion,

shouting

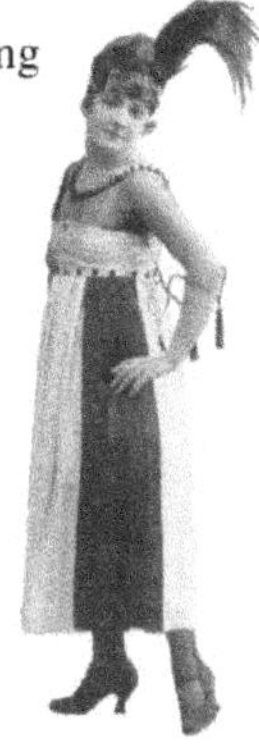

and acting

ever ready to push the social
envelope
to some unique personality trait,

to be judged in turn with feigned
shock and laughter

by others.

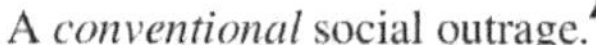

A *conventional* social outrage.

Waving at a car

for example.

Of course ....→ not everyone

is like

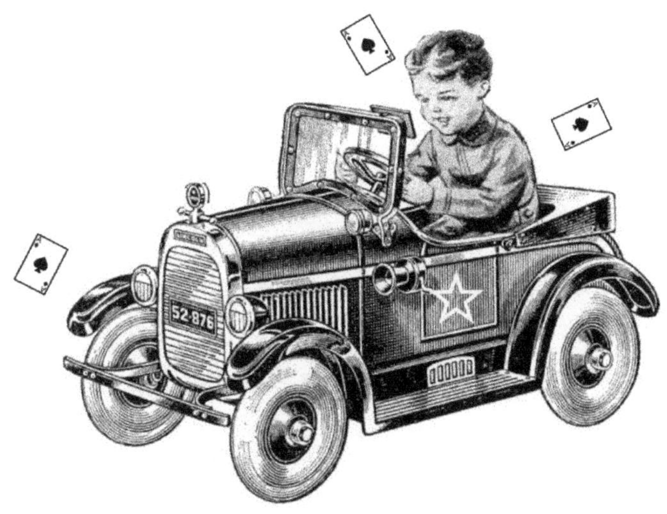

t*h*a*t

•

And not:

☒ everyone,
☐ crackheads,
☐ shoppers,
☒ walkers about,

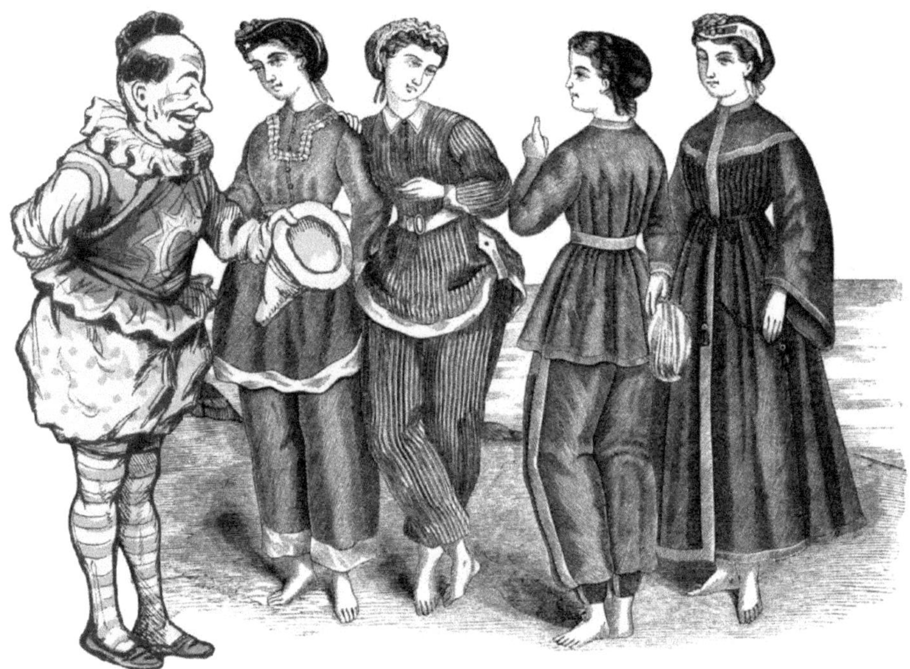

☐ children's dresses,
☒ drivers

are eagerly looking for the social norm

and are **not** wanting to be **im**polite
to the peer group.

But the waitresses. !

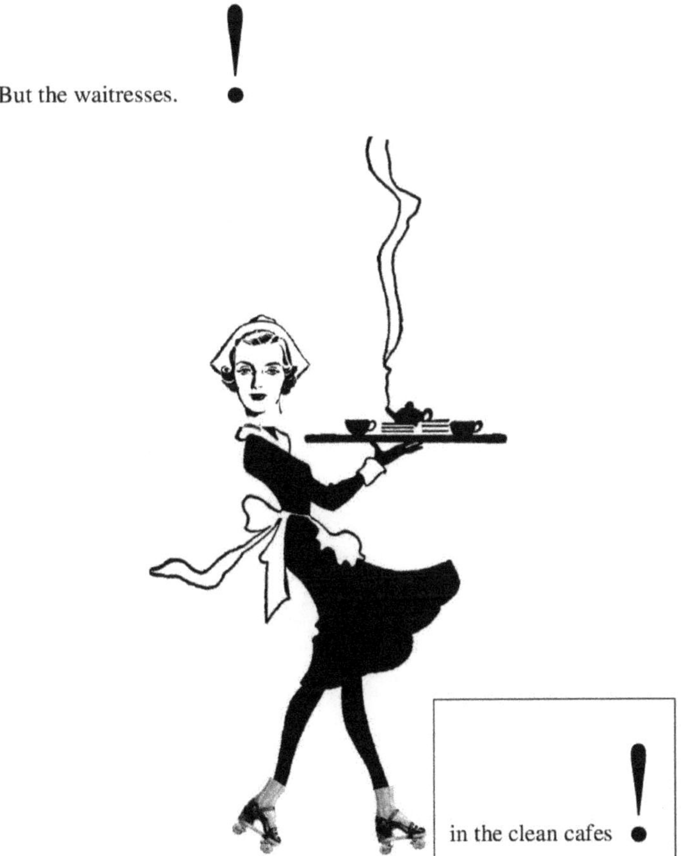

in the clean cafes !

are as eager to please as a London prostitute

in great praise of your choice!

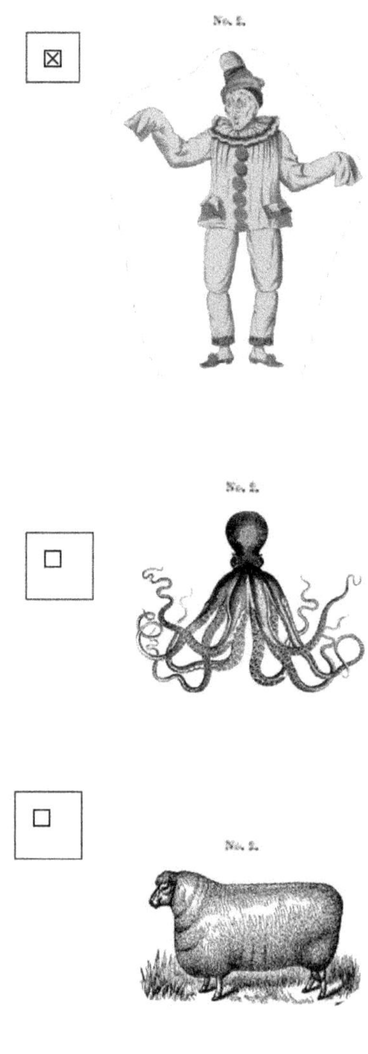

Number 2, perhaps?

Everything is perfect! brilliant!
an excellent choice

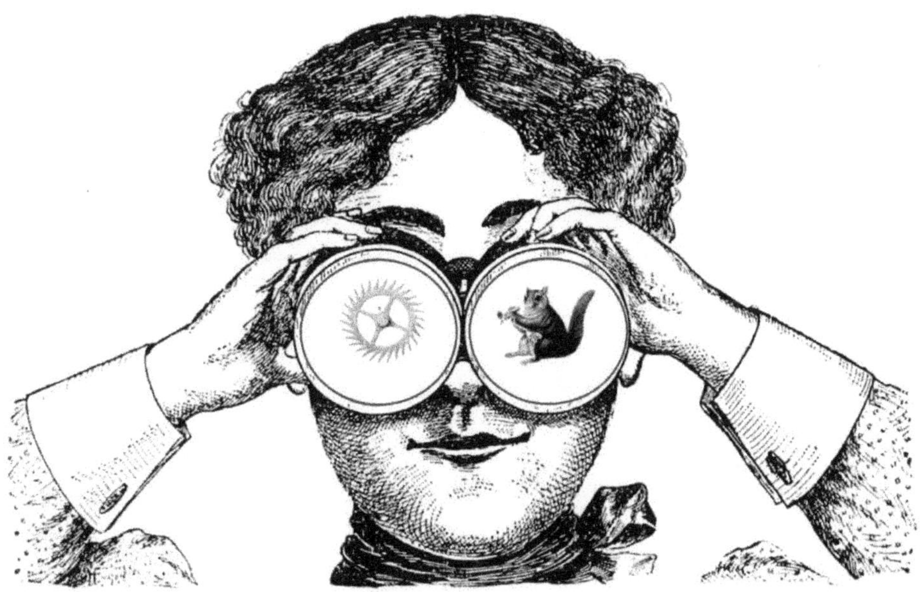

Like Vancouver itself.

Or?

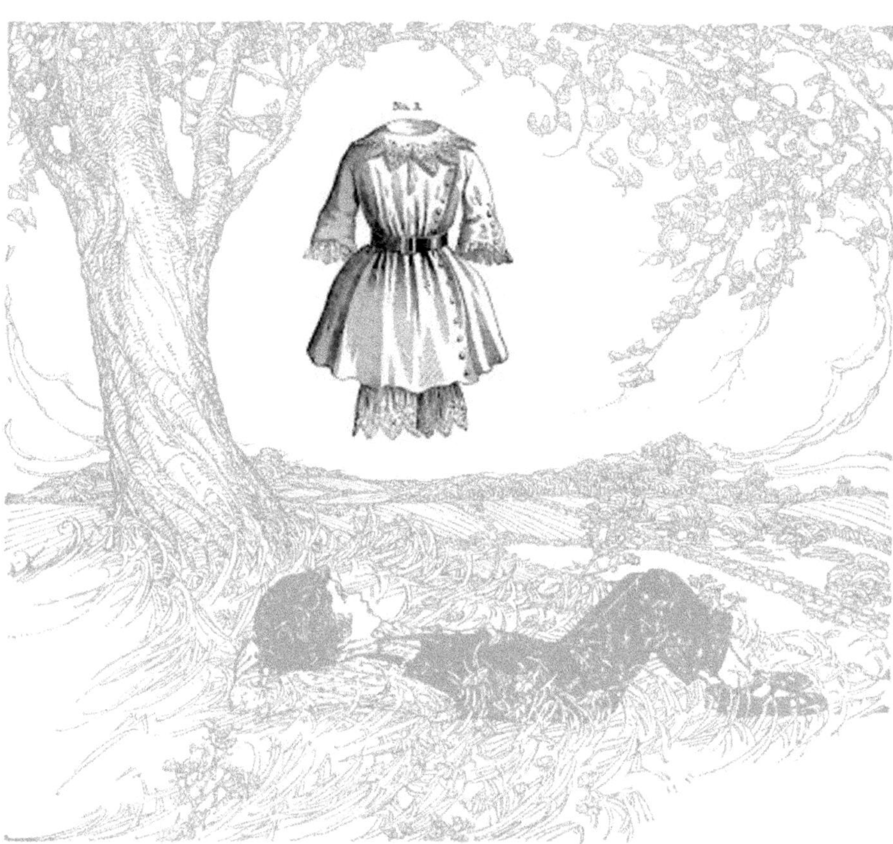

It seems a land of eternally unfulfilled but promised summer

not like Lond⚽□n

where everything has just been

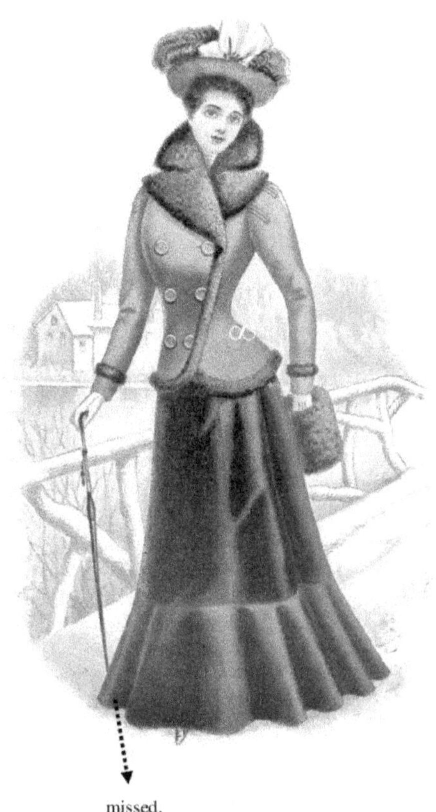

missed.

It seems a land where something must be going on somewhere else,
somewhere perfect,

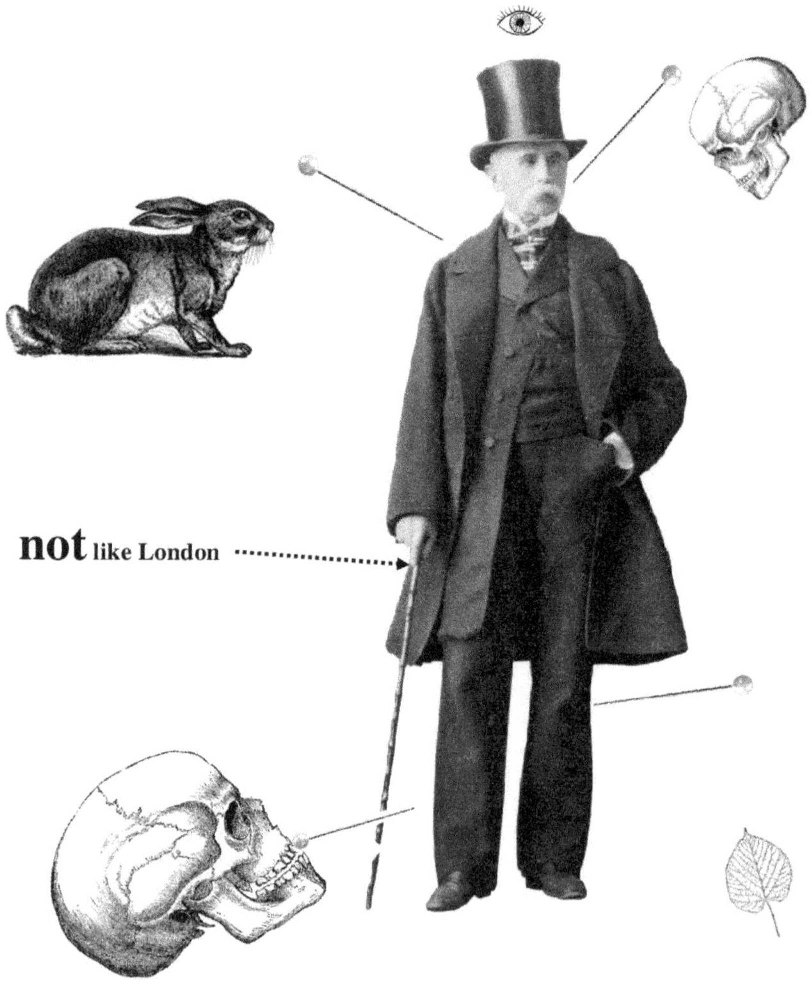

where you can always see some

T*H*I*N*G

in the:

Everything

road ahead you should avoid.

in both

places

is

just

the one of pleasant ness

less than ideal:

and the other one of dark renaissance

and everything therefore

is soon forgotten

like Gwen Pharis outside of William's Lake.

Of course,

Gwen was born into the U.S.
and although she was at a Prairie University □□
she never became one of the tenured brand names
of that particular cult to be o b i t u a r i z e d
by her generation and the next for points. In

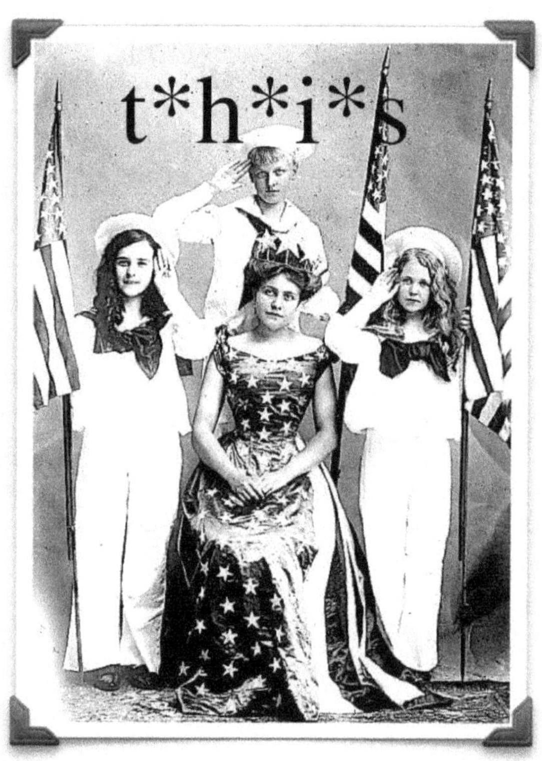

she is like the dead poet here
in one respect:

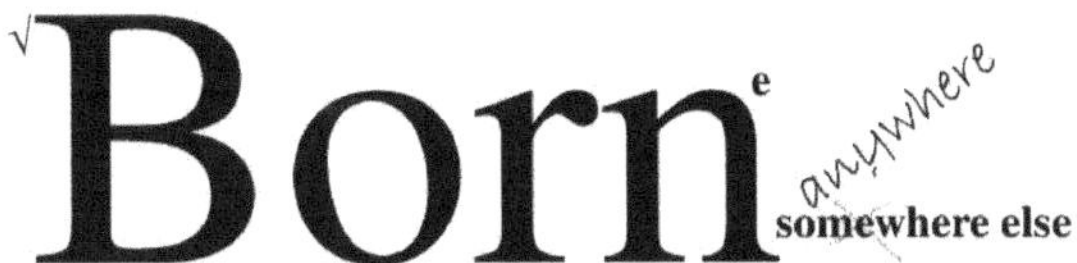

and part of **another** locality

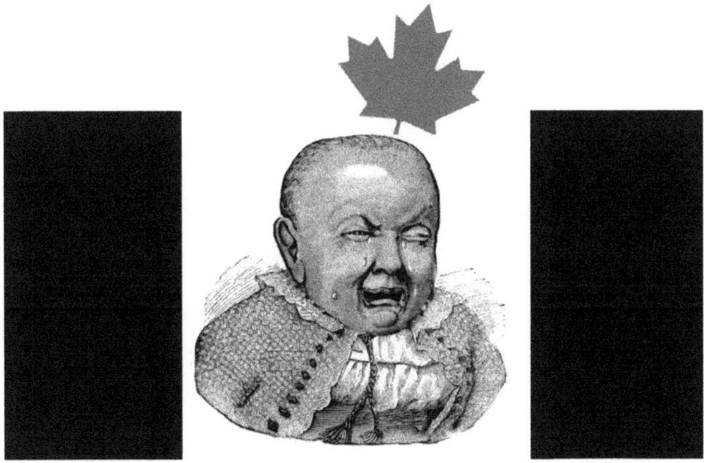

by way of liter-ary integration.

Good for her,

for:

like every rite writer,

she is both

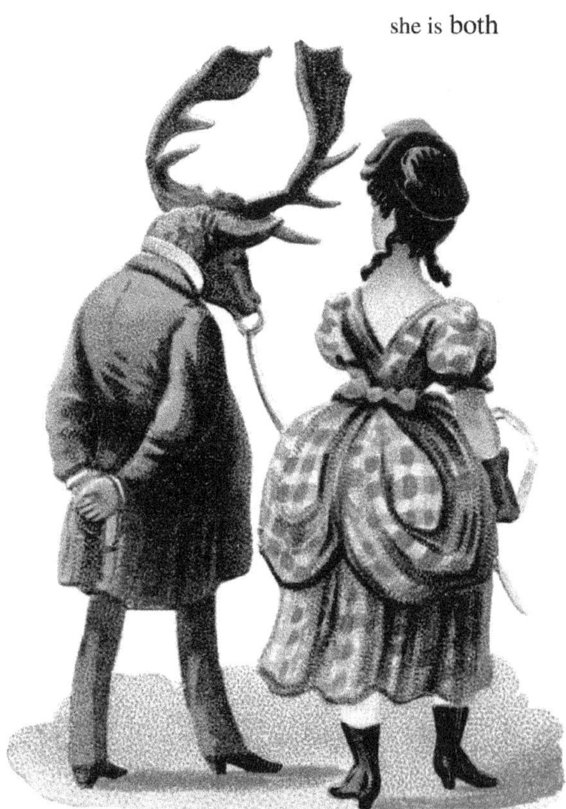

a su¢¢ess and a <u>failure.</u>

And many do it in this way.

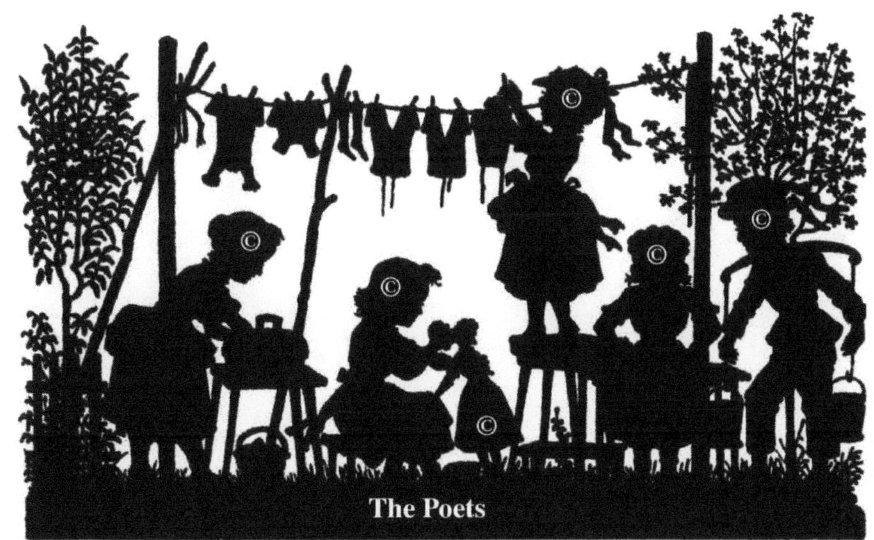

in ©ompanions to literature in

Canada

usually

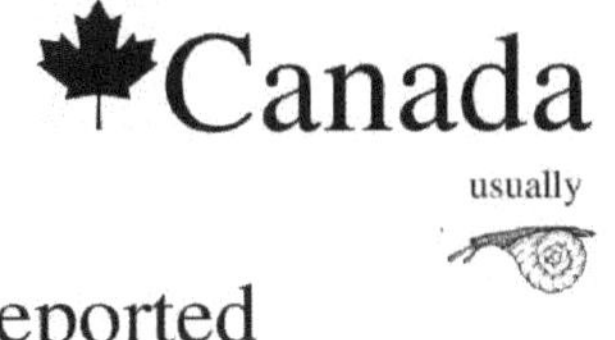

are reported

in the early post-British colonial

crop

as having birth places in

England,

an infancy there,

or a

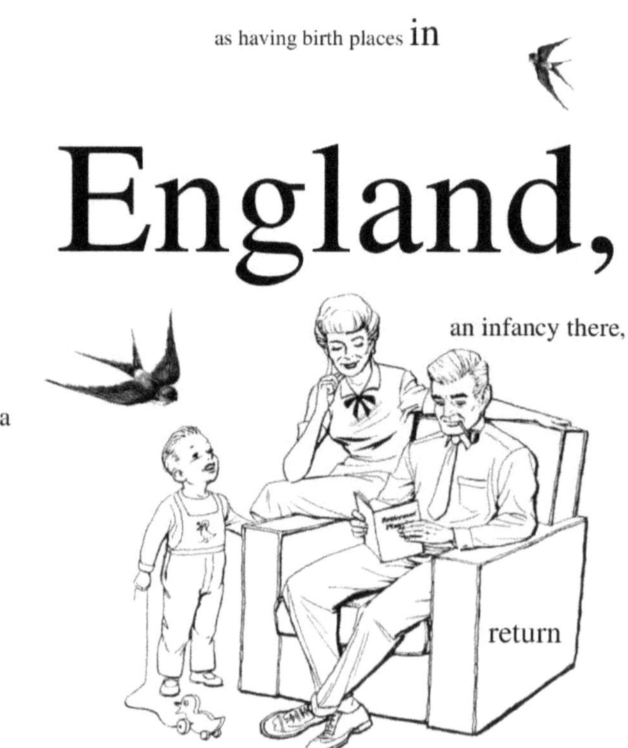

return

.

Some,
but not many,
are actual immigrants from other places,

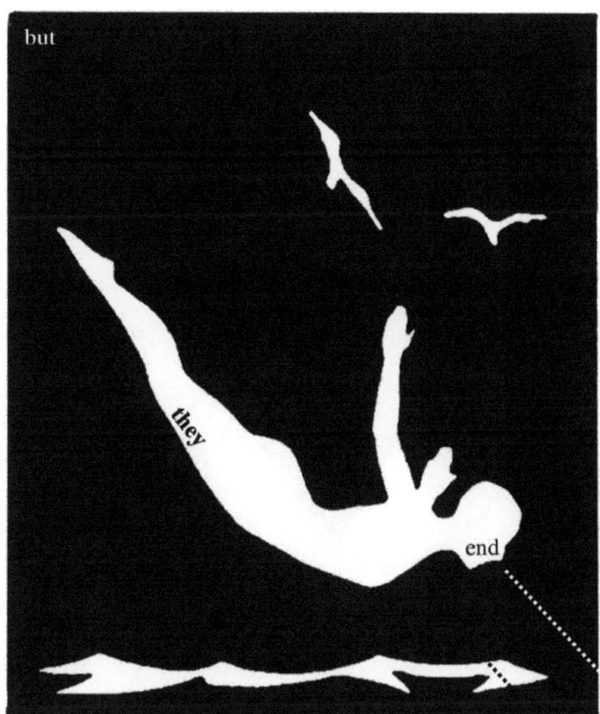

dn

being

not seminal in the development of. things.

One or two are indigenes

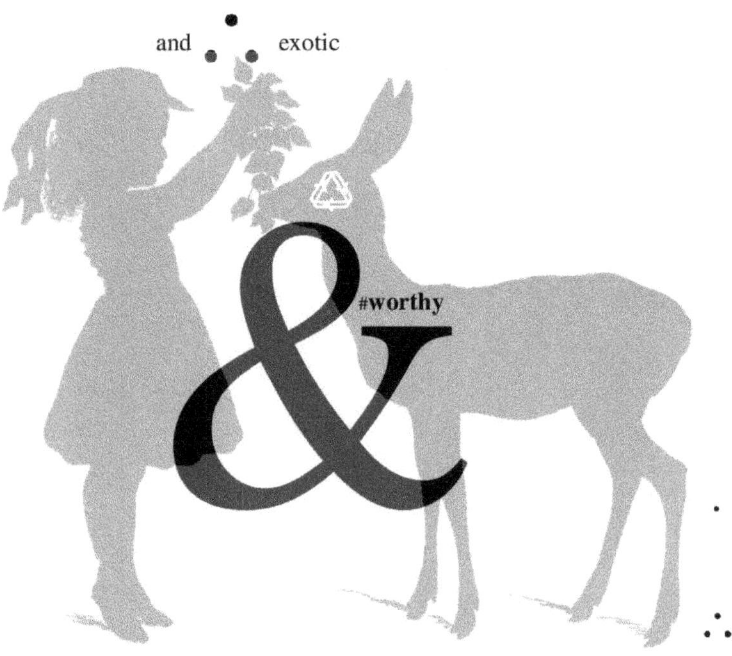

There **are** a few in the early crop

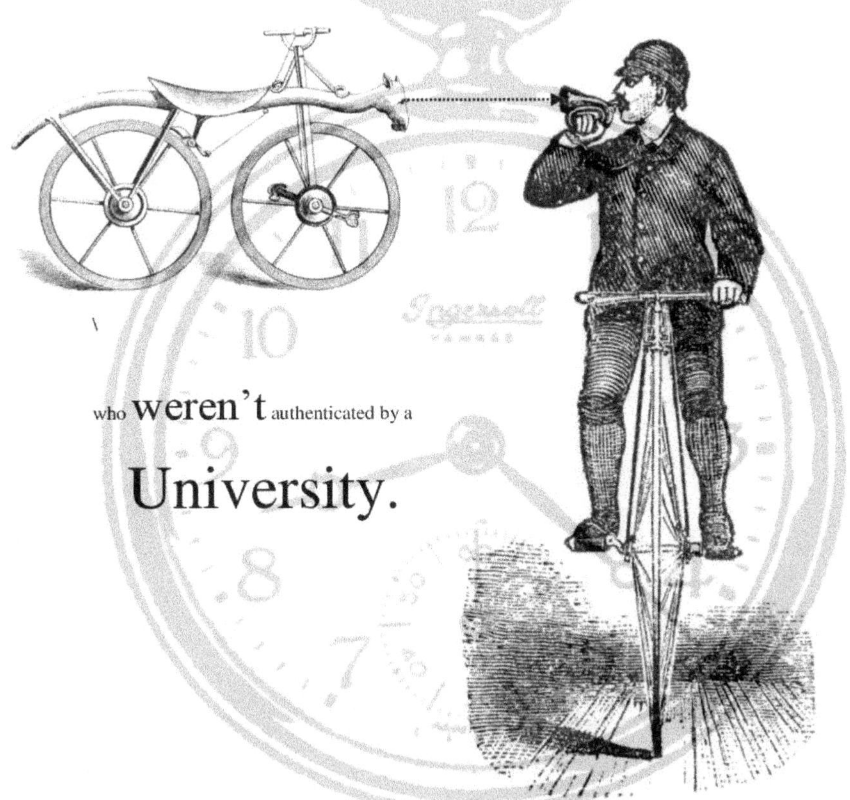

who weren't authenticated by a

University.

The contraries,

the ones

who came and lived

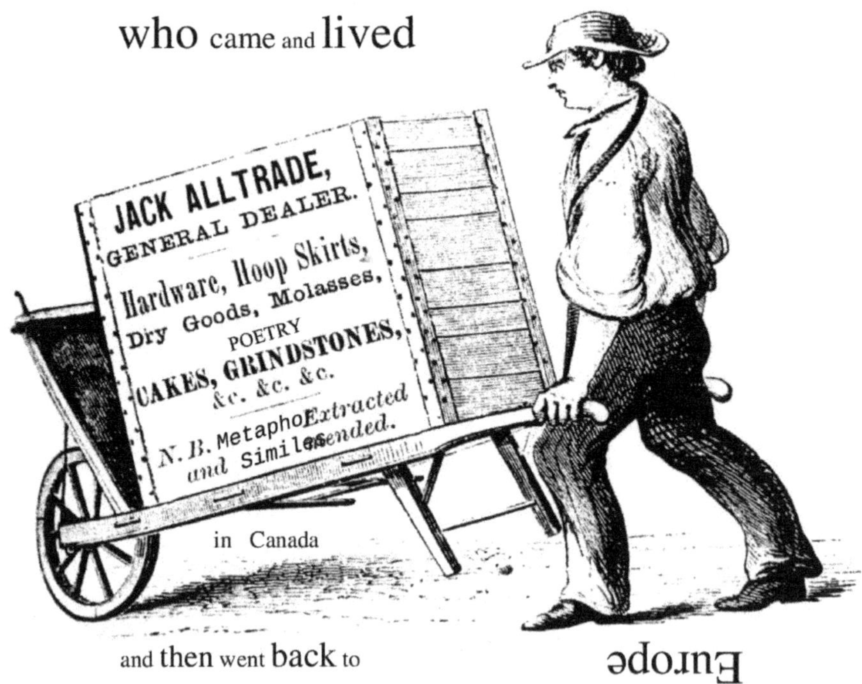

in Canada

and then went back to Europe

are hardly mentioned at all.

The newer more American

crop is mentioned

with other parameters

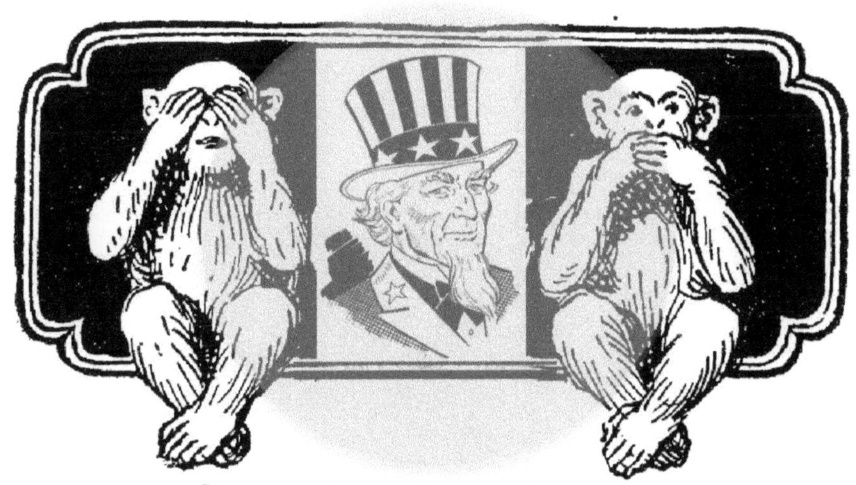

T*his

is usually by city and the social

spheres.

And now I start to think of those ~~real~~ American

Americans.

Hey!

What about William Logan's book
of Poetry criticism

'Our Savage Art',

eh.

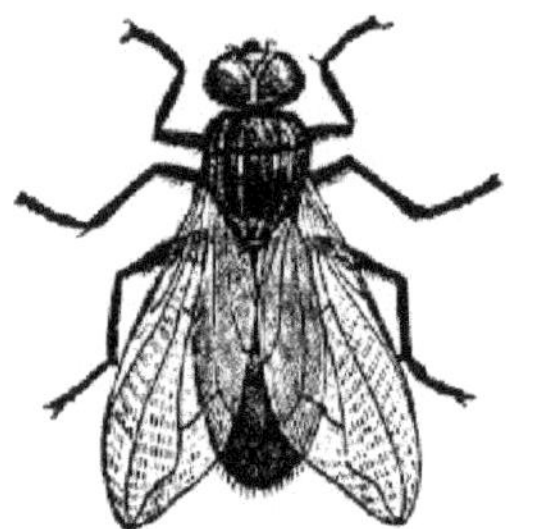

He

writes of writers,
especially poets,

be/coming

‘cartoon mascots

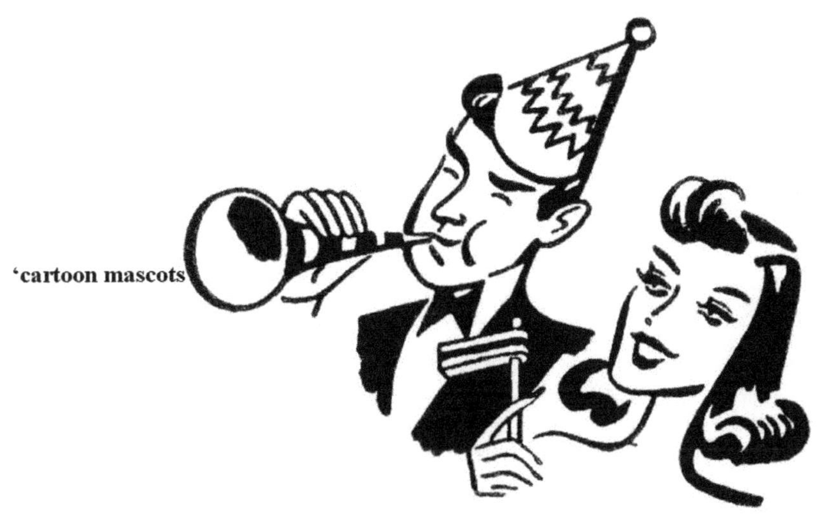

of such things
as their

☒ ethnicities,
☒ races,
☒ aesthetics,
☒ classes and
☐ sexualities

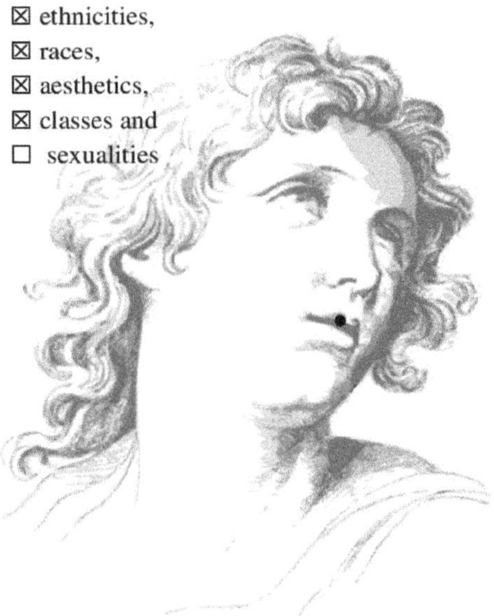

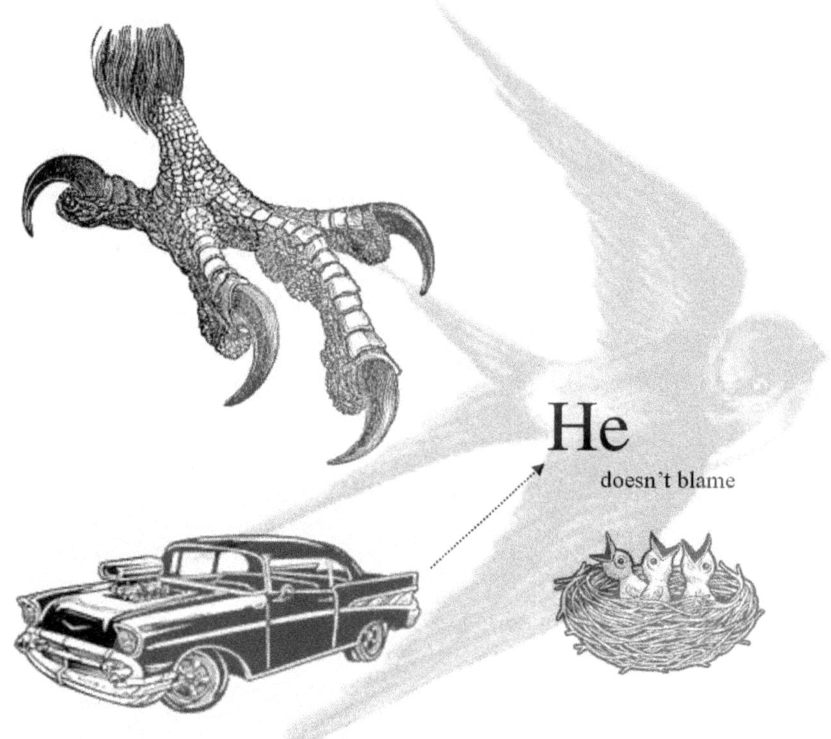

United States Culture

which makes all that entirely
official,
as I would.

Nor does he blame

the style of

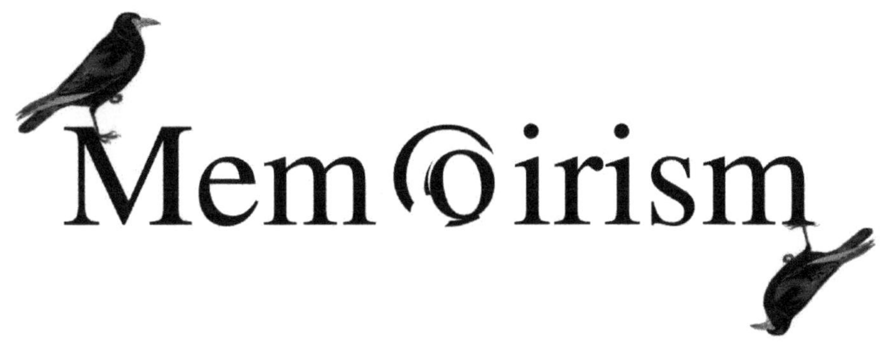

which is tied into

☒ eDevices,
☒ webs and
☒ twitters,

as I would

but I think he proves it with reference to

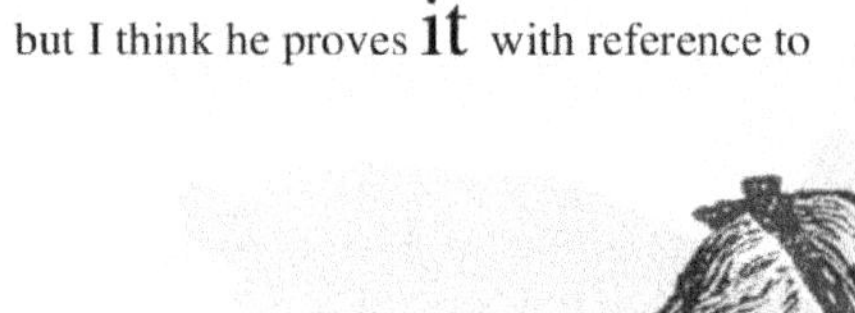

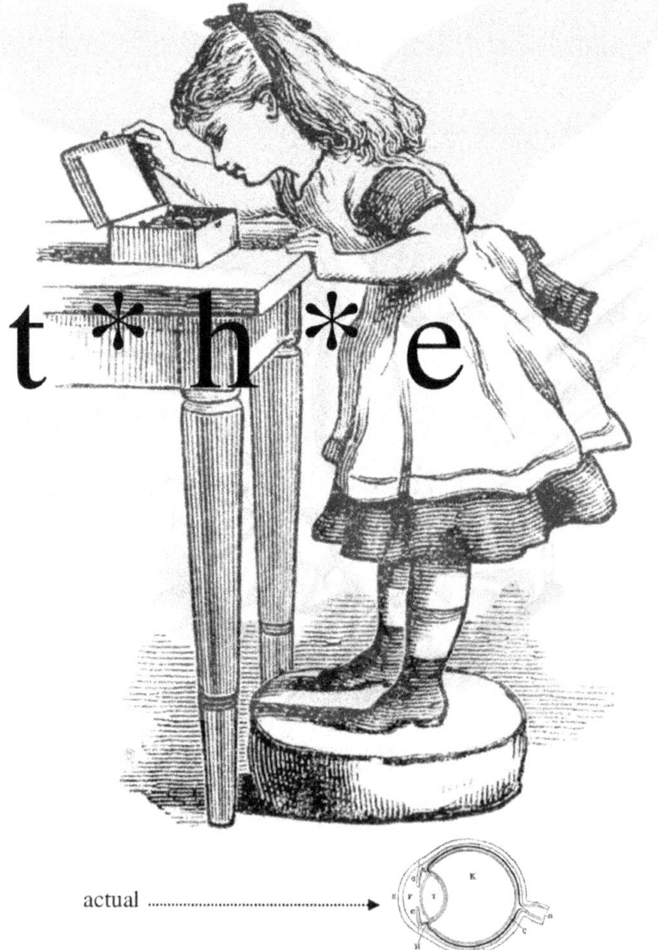

t*h*e

actual ……………………………………→

And now at this point in the Wake

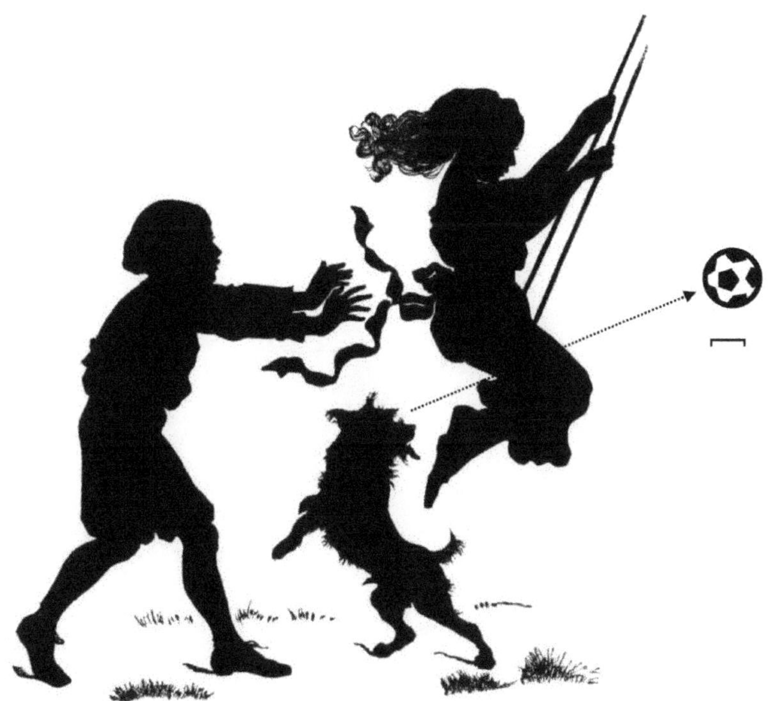

as the poor dead poet's soul travels onward
and its body is about to be dumped into a suburban grave,

with great embarrassment

and contrary to the passion of my youth,

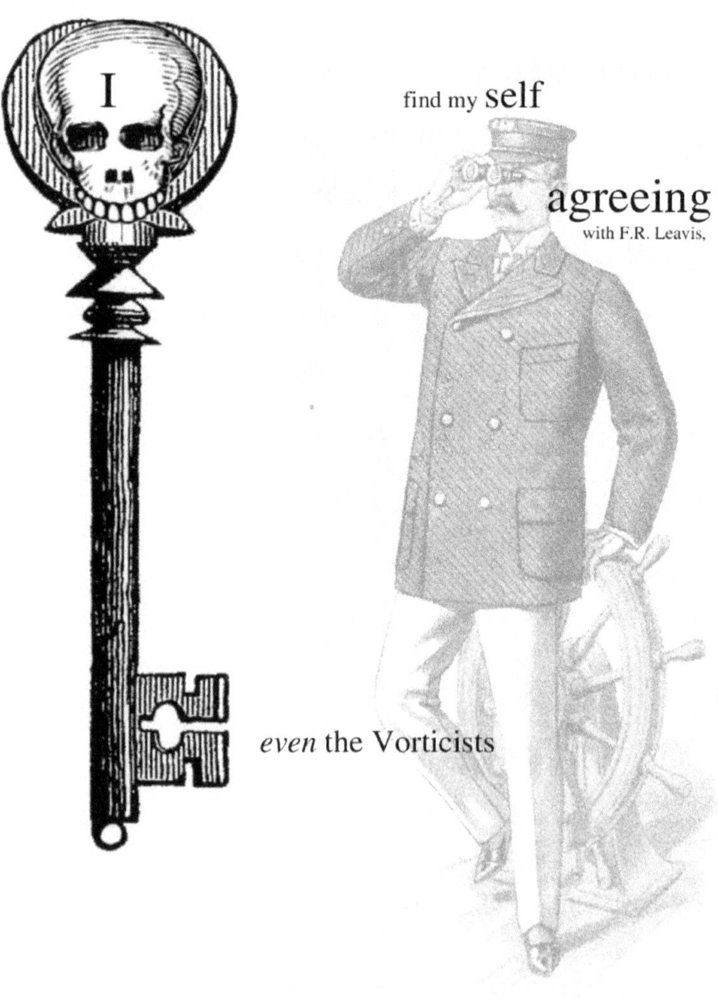

I

find my self

agreeing

with F.R. Leavis,

even the Vorticists

,

against the excitement

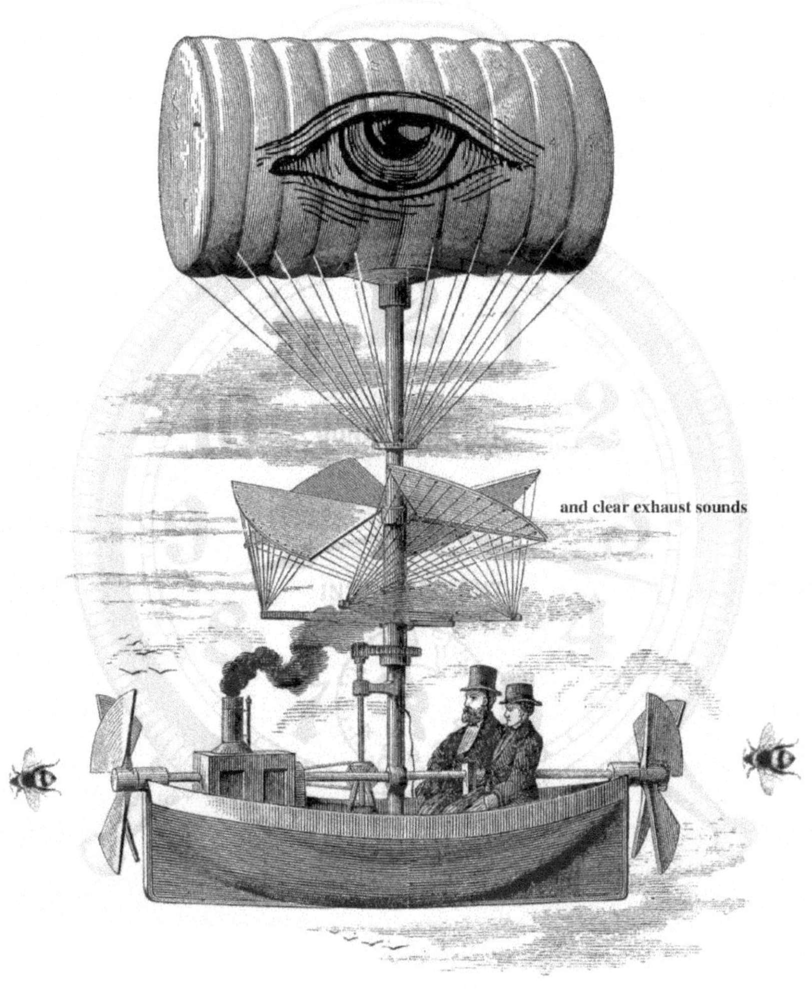

of the Futurists.

I am eating a piece of the fish

and the hearse has stopped

where Leavis deplored the decline of humanitarian

and moral

literature with the advent of

what is now

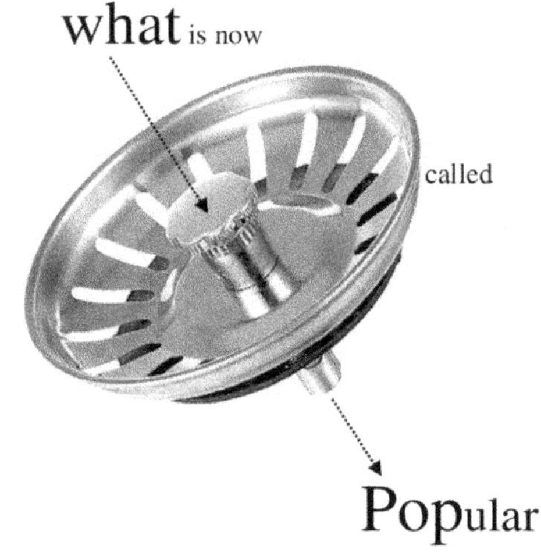

called

Popular.

Because it is all going you know.

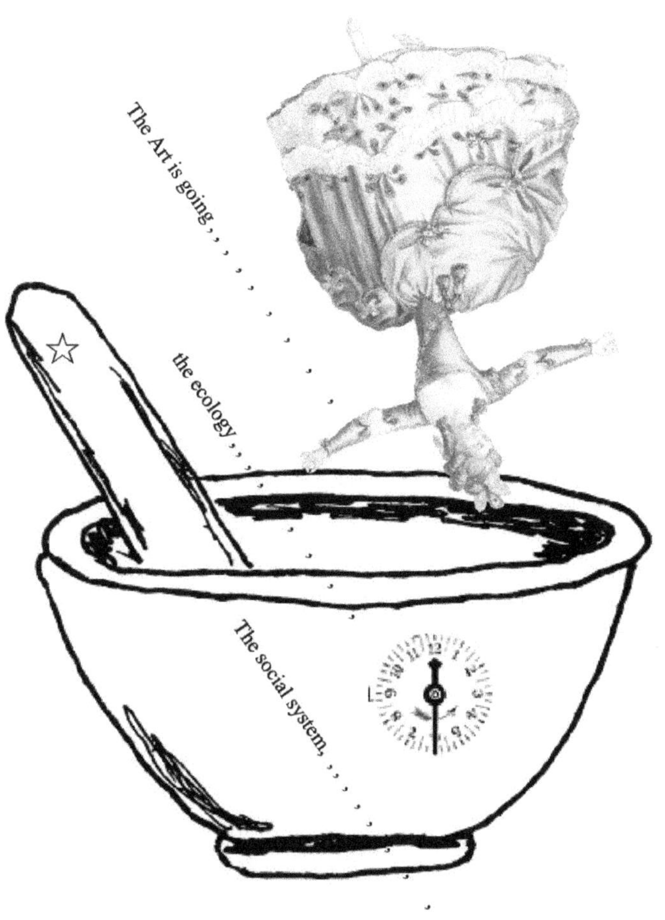
The Art is going . . . .
the ecology . . . .
The social system, ...

I rage

to my self

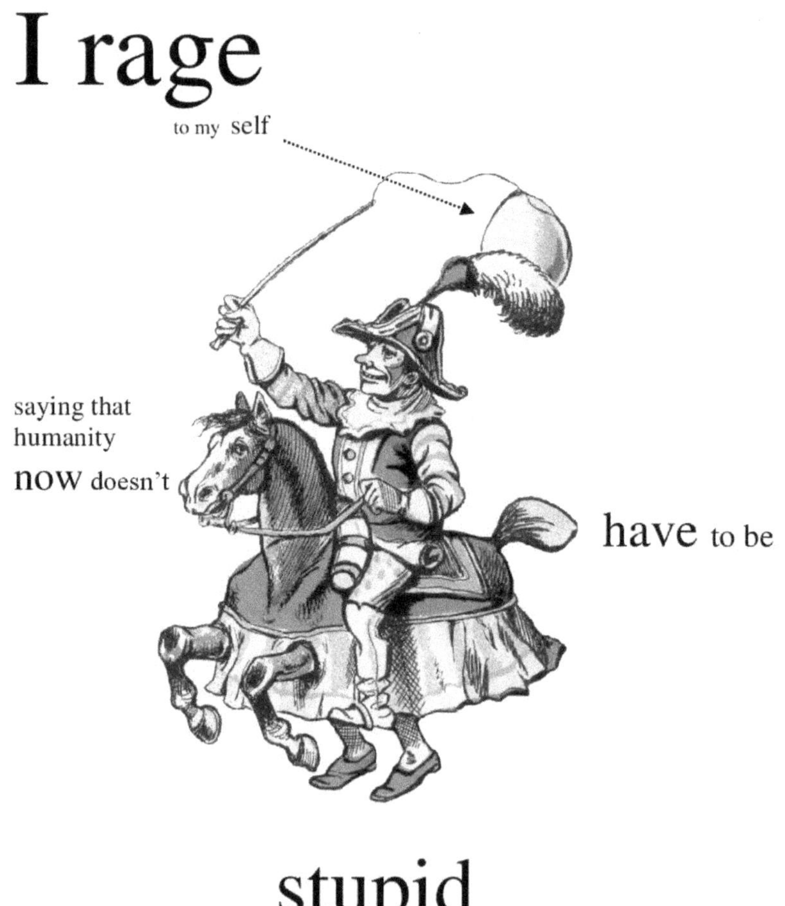

saying that
humanity
now doesn't

have to be

stupid

.sepytoerets fo maerd a ni dna   and in a dream of stereotypes.

It

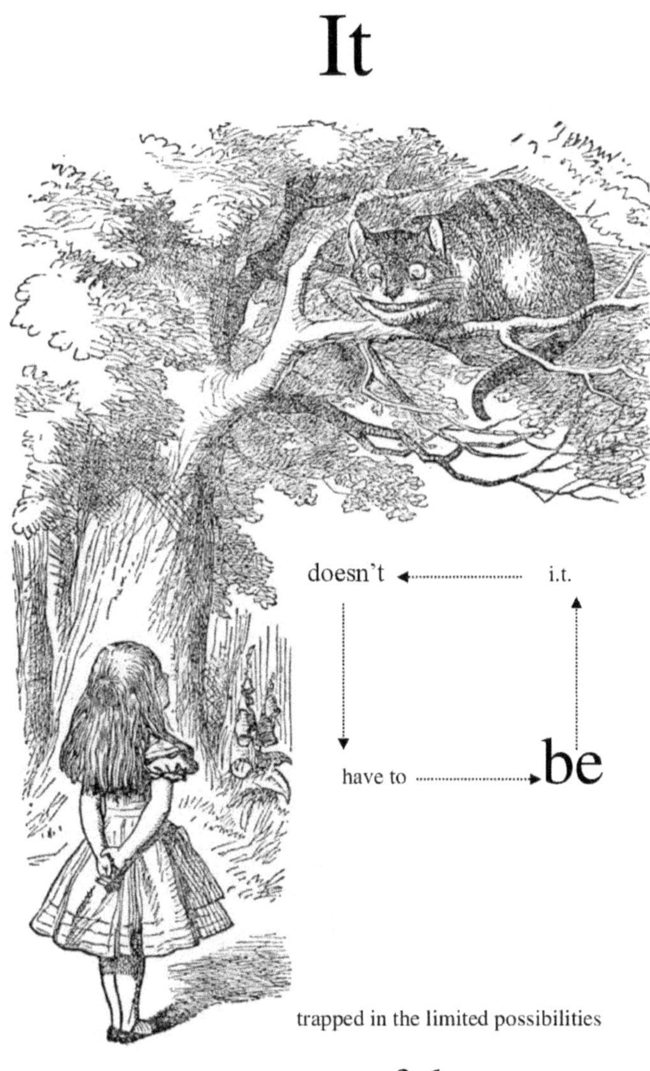

doesn't ← i.t.

have to → be

trapped in the limited possibilities

of **false** oppositions

in 2-dimensional information.

I choke a little on a cookie

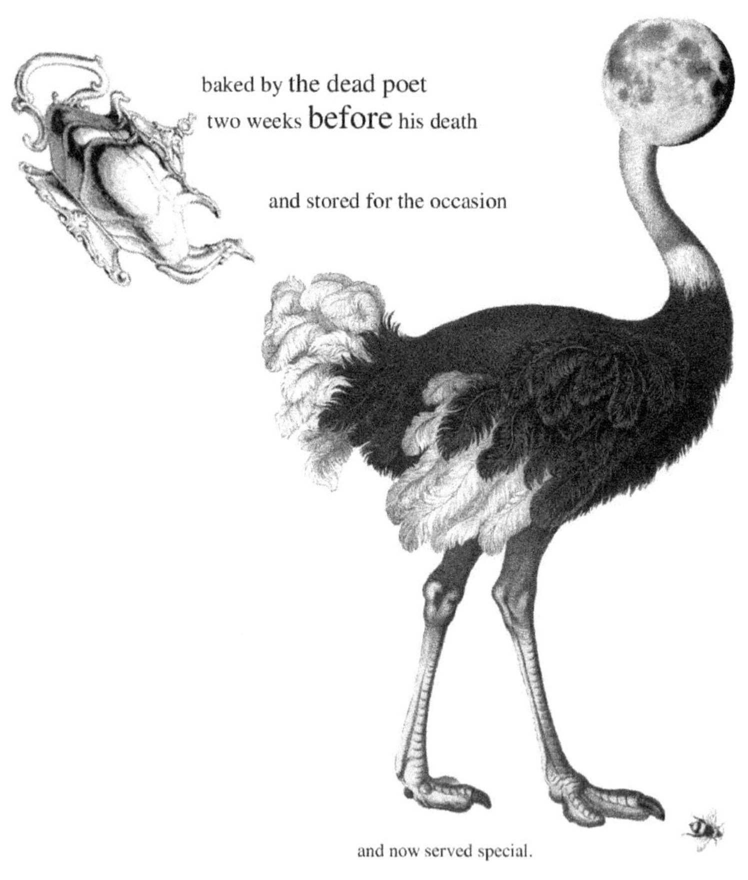

baked by the dead poet
two weeks before his death

and stored for the occasion

and now served special.

There is
a packet (half smoked) of his cigarettes
on the banister.

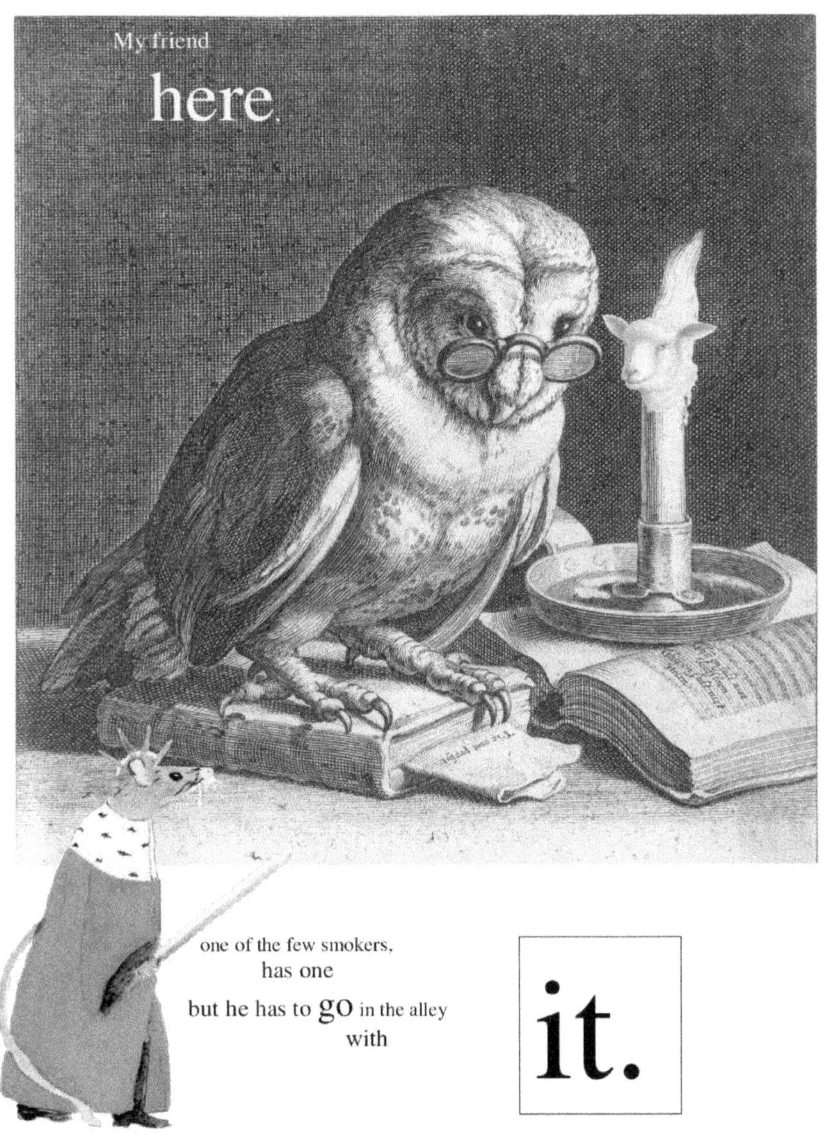

one of the few smokers,
has one
but he has to go in the alley
with

it.

The chatterbox looks at me and says:

☒ 'You are
☐ very
☒ flamboyant'

He asks for some more of my books.

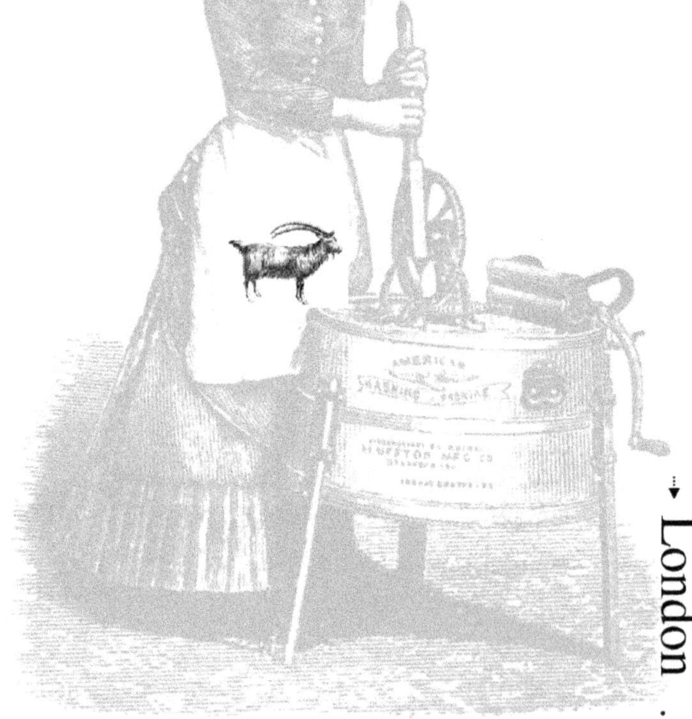

London.

He wishes to come to my place in

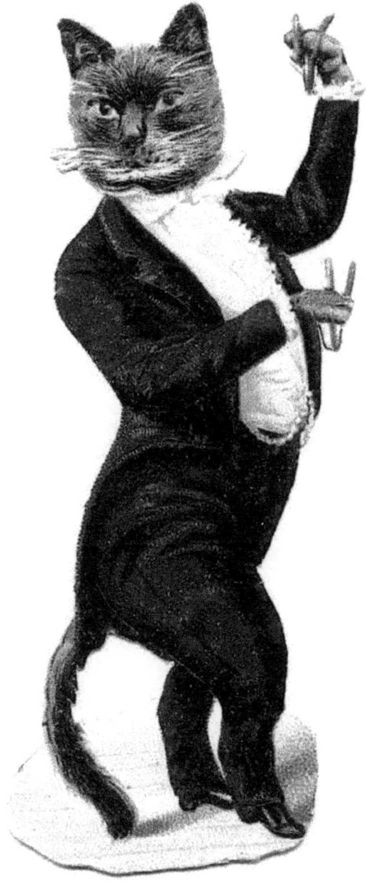

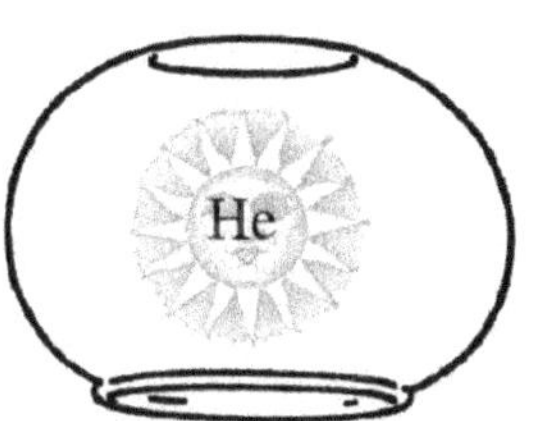

lectures there sometimes

as he has developed his old

British market
with

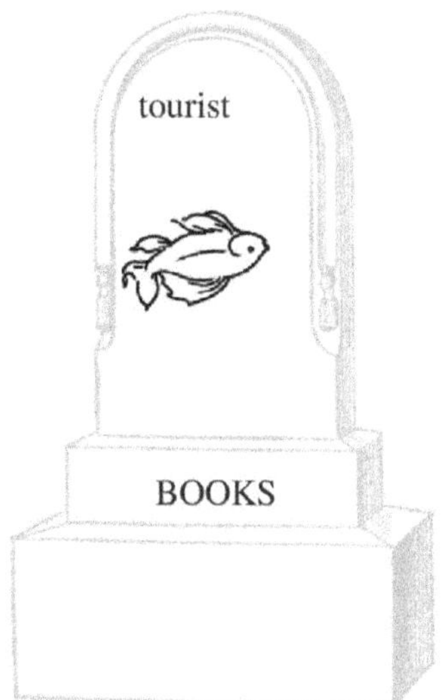

He is mistaken
as others have been
if he thinks he can return
from the dead ,

with him getting me

admission to the cemetery

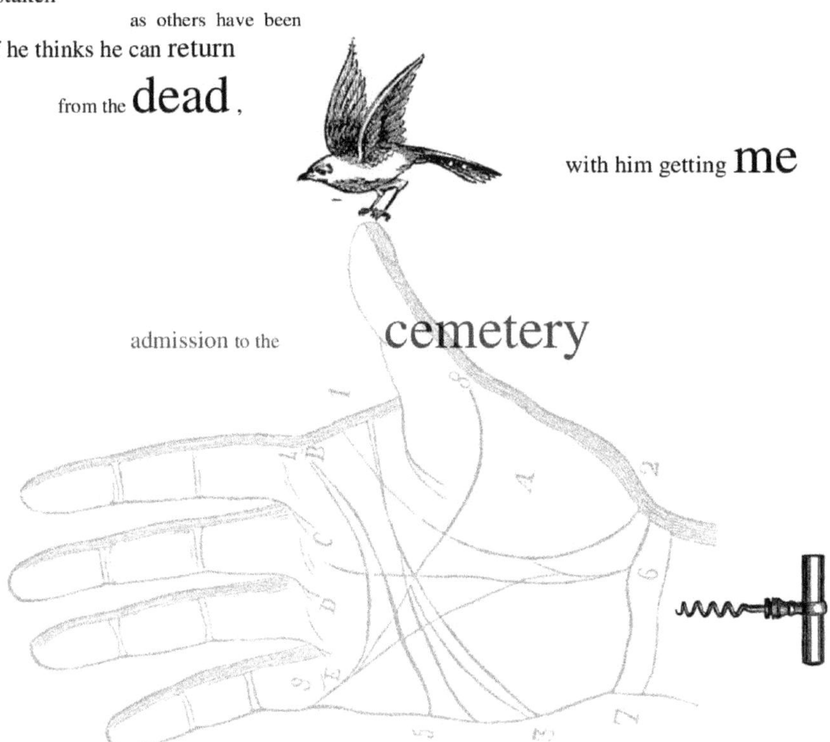

I never will be able to do

t * h * a * t * .

He had best go back to his other obituaries

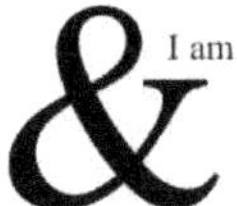
I am

nothing special

because of London and France and the Balkan

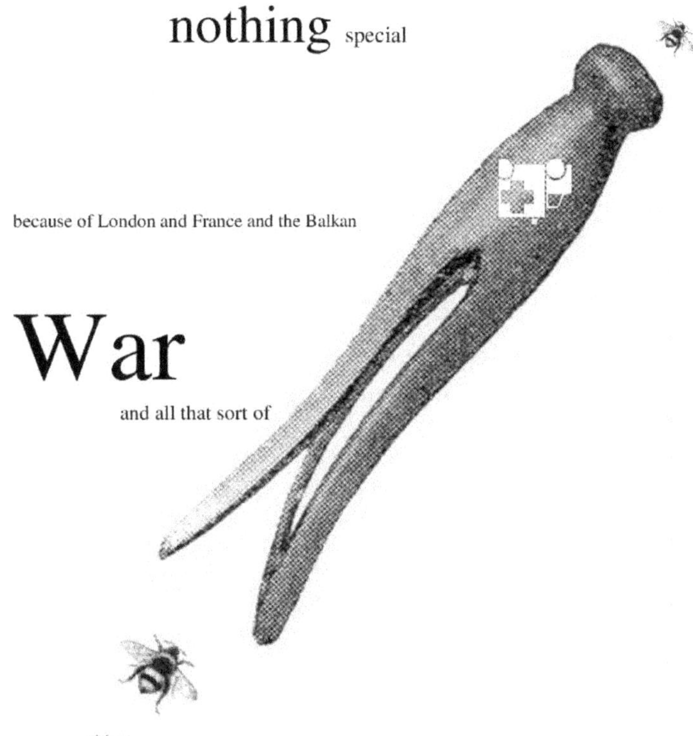

War

and all that sort of

thing

because that is actually pretty

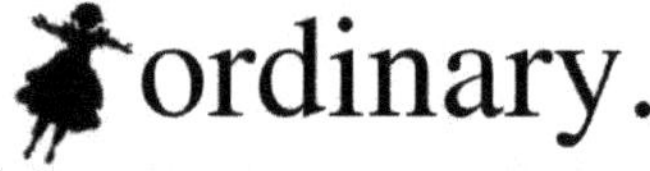

ordinary.

It is this kind of place which is not.

This eternal quiet back yard of catered wake.

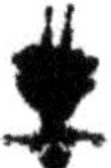

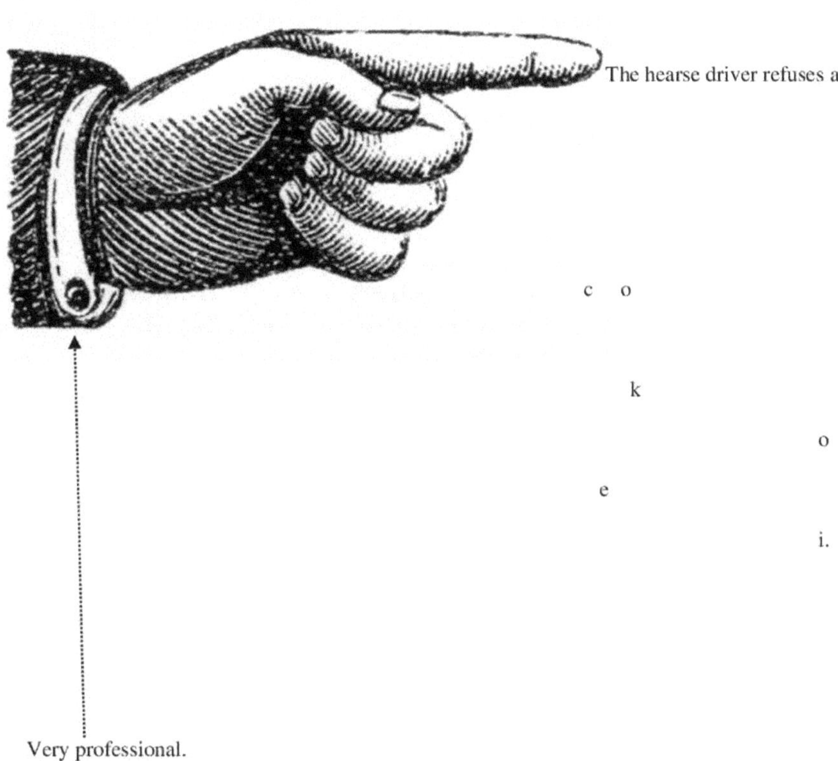
The hearse driver refuses a
c o
k
o
e
i.
Very professional.

Good

God,

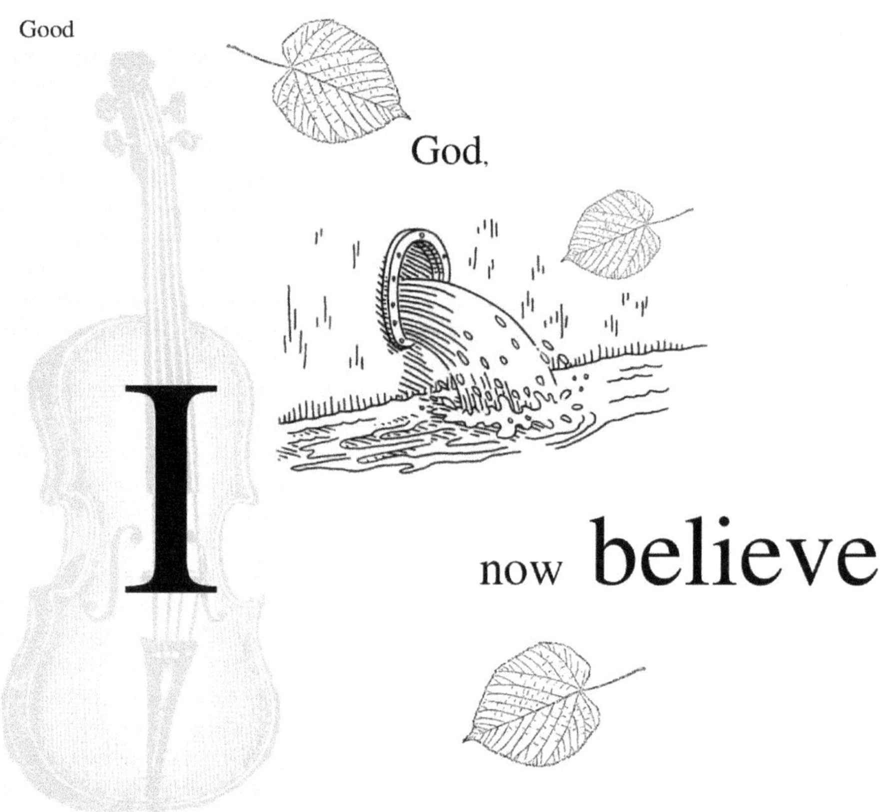

I

now believe

in respect for the dead.

There was that famous encounter
in a seminar in Eastern Europe

where

Michael Ondaatje had spoken as an erudite
☒ writer,
☒ lecturer and
☐ internationalist Canadian

on the nature of ~~cults~~ culture
and his critique of

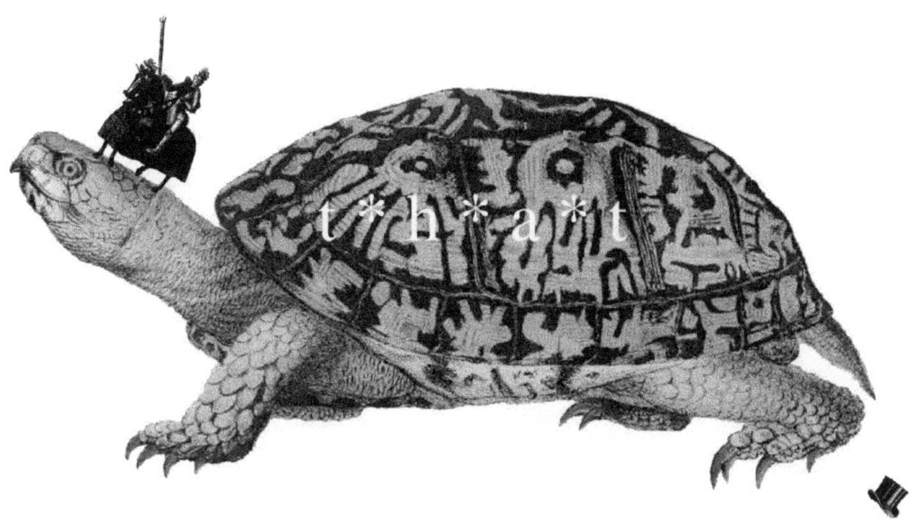

in the Nationalists
he had met.

A poet

with a wonderful name shouted at him and said:

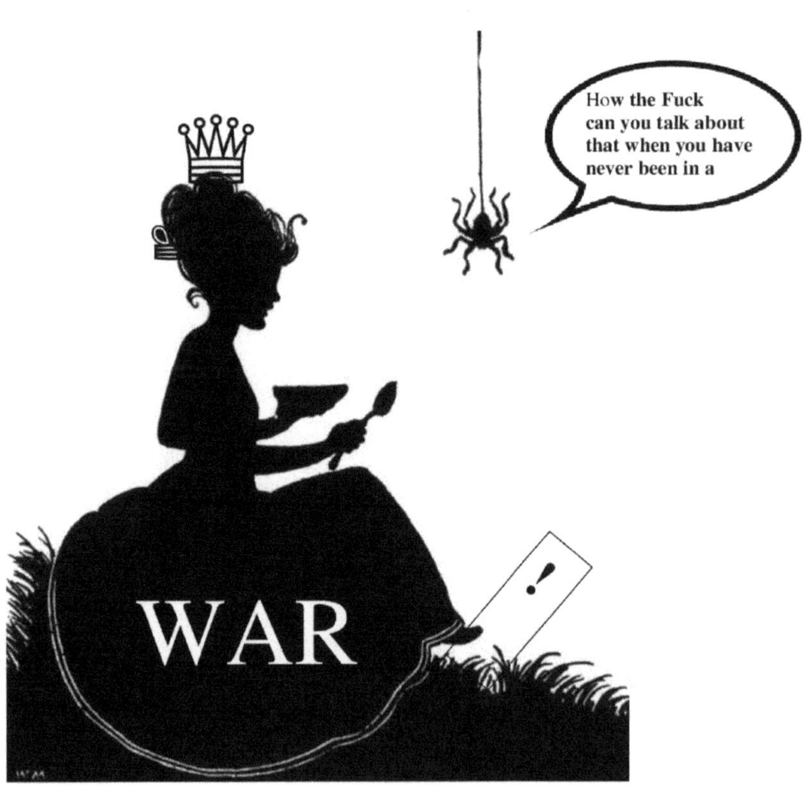

Ondaatje

walked off the stage

dramatically

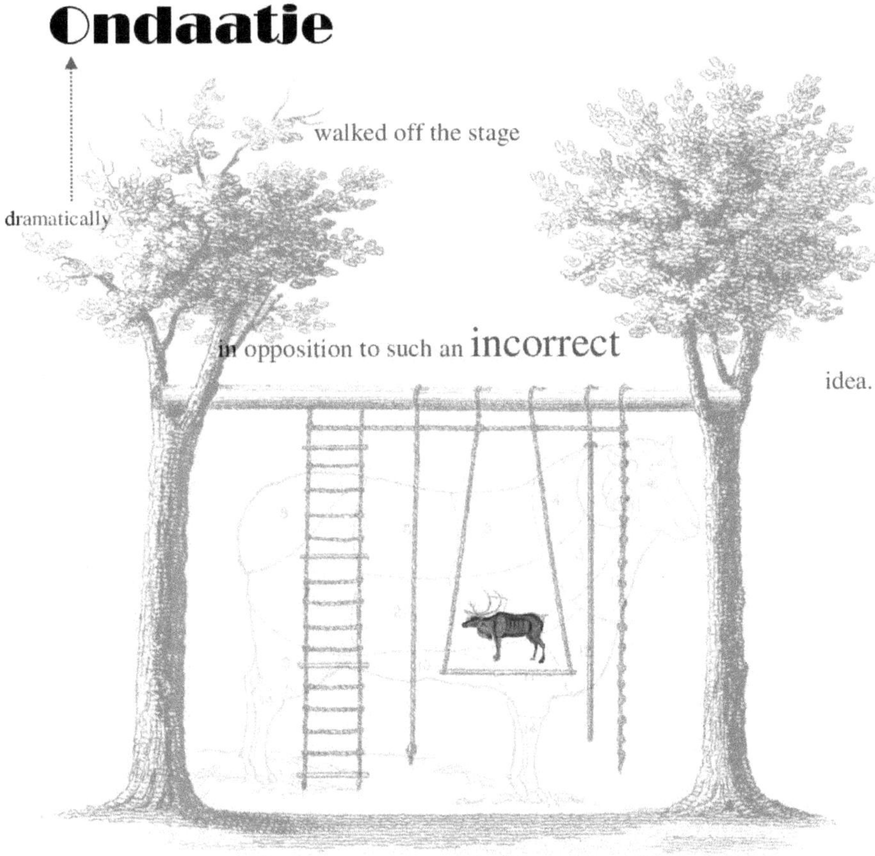

in opposition to such an incorrect

idea.

He is a Canadian after all.

I believe in him.

And also in Alien abduction.

For:

☒ I have heard you all here
☐ and have read you
☒ lately
☒ and this is not the personalities
☐ and minds
☒ that were here when the idea was to break through dreaming
☐ and forget the consequence.

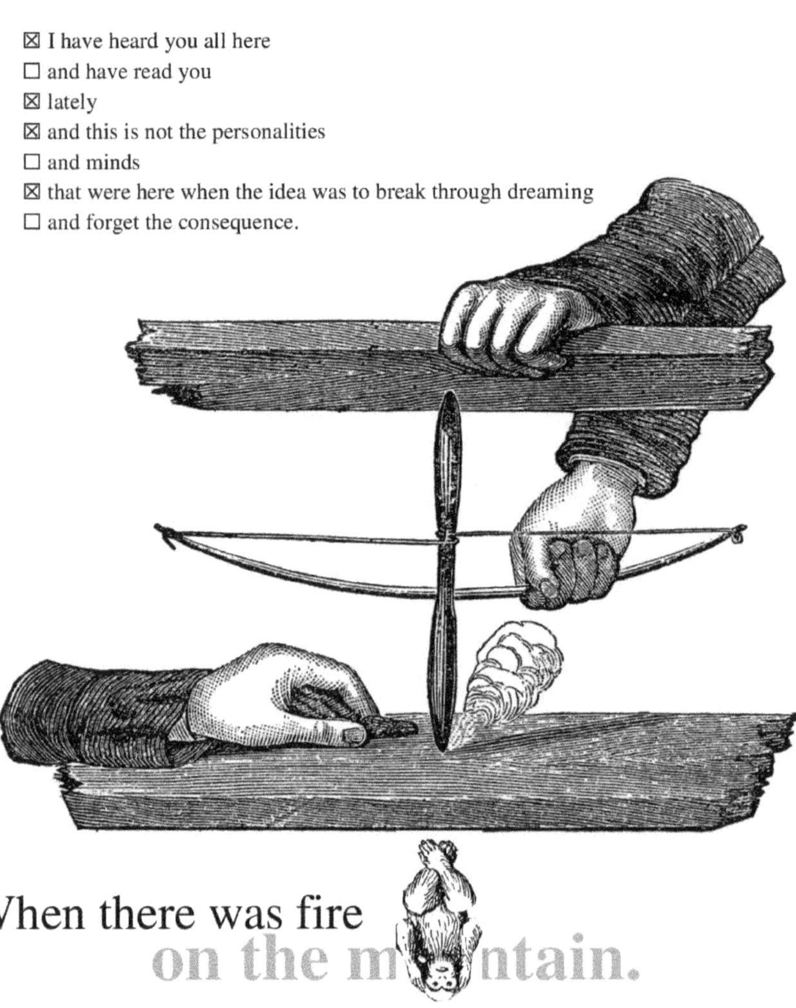

When there was fire
on the m ntain.
ou

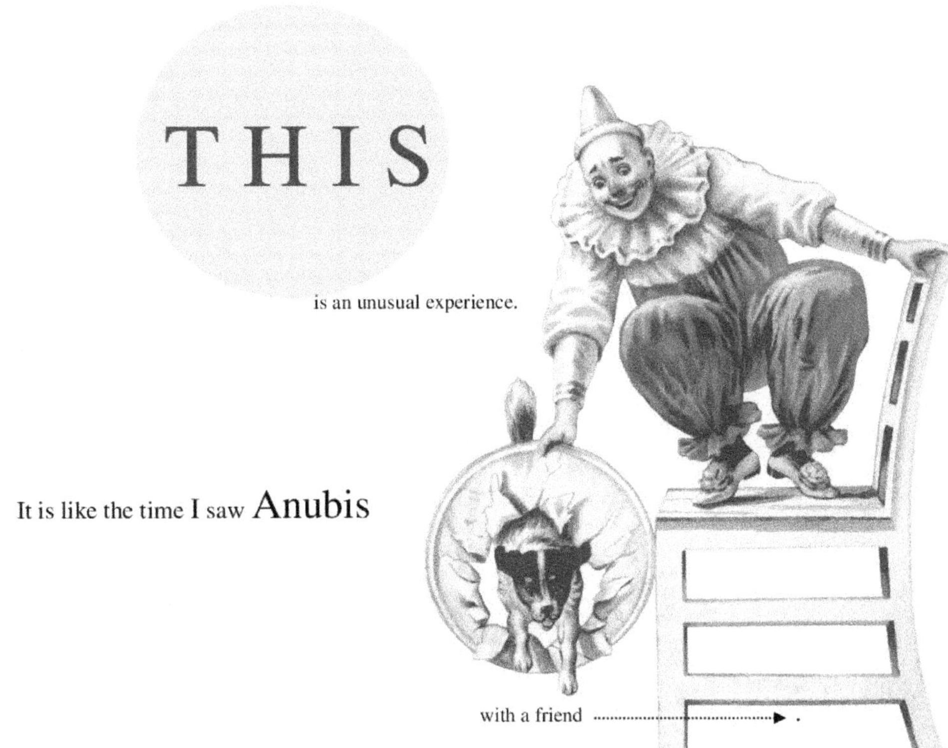

THIS

is an unusual experience.

It is like the time I saw Anubis

with a friend ▸ .

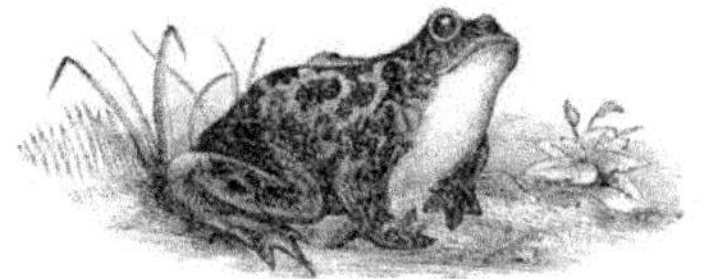

There is a poetess here

of alarming superficiality

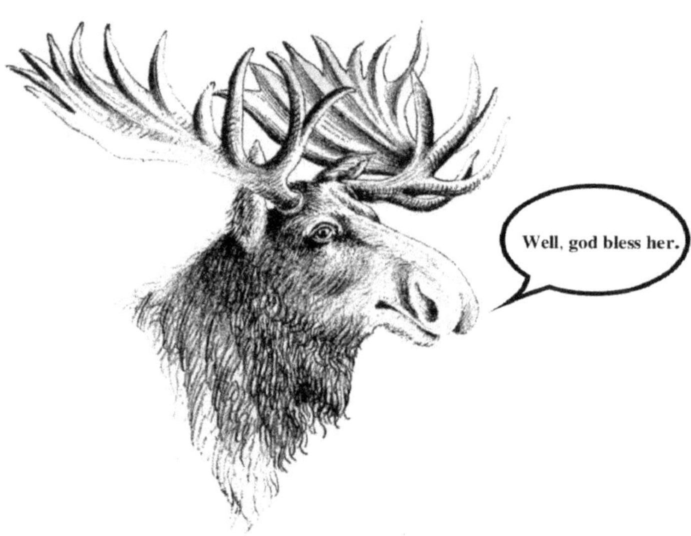

but convinced of her unique taste

and mission of self-assertion.

There is a department head here,

the ~~second~~ third one from the one I knew

I knew this one as a risk adverse student,
but

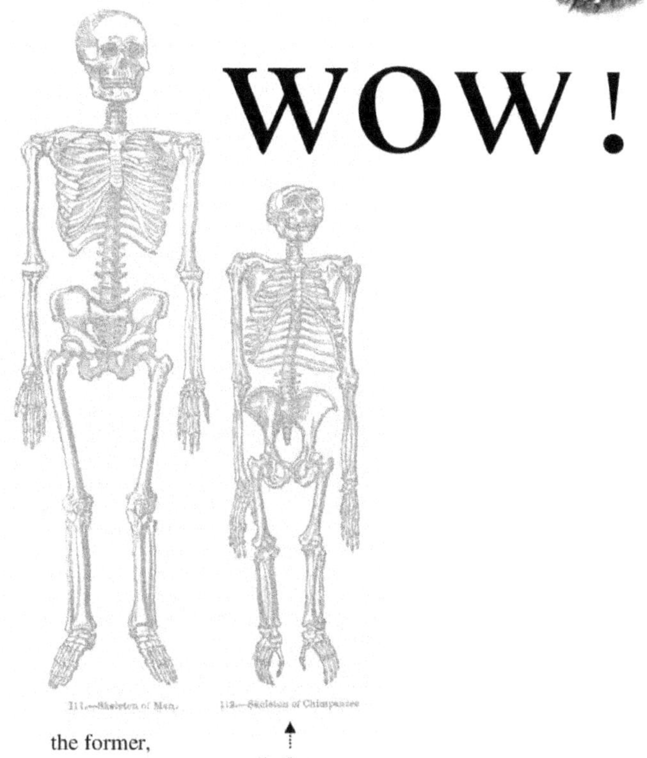

WOW!

the former,

the first,

the one who did exegesis
for hours
mutilating Shakespeare
in the privacy of his room!

This one looks at me for an instant;
eyes narrowed with suspicion

and asks

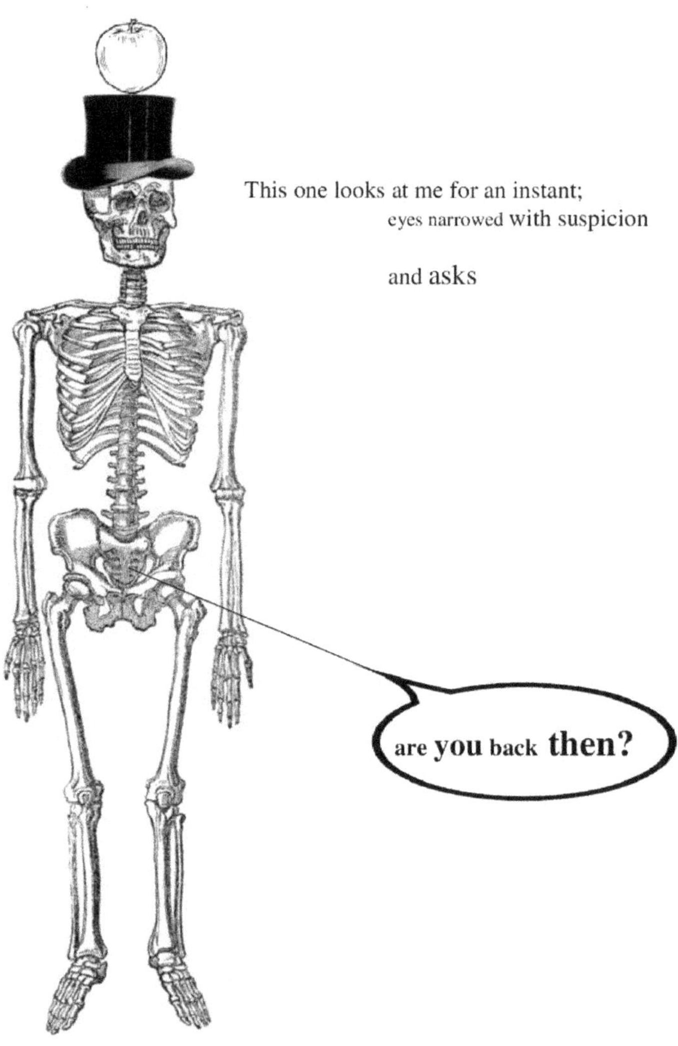

I say: I live in France
when not in London.

I am not from here

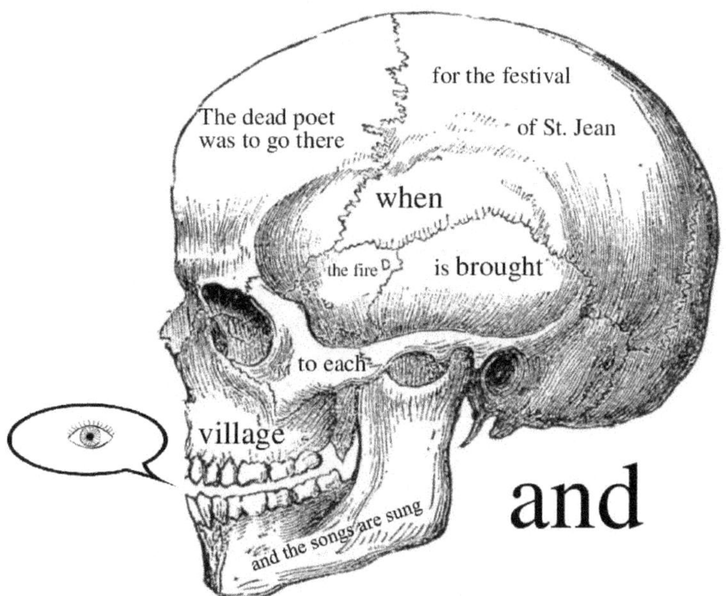

and

the dance of the dead begins at midnight

I am not,

and I wouldn't think of it ever as back.

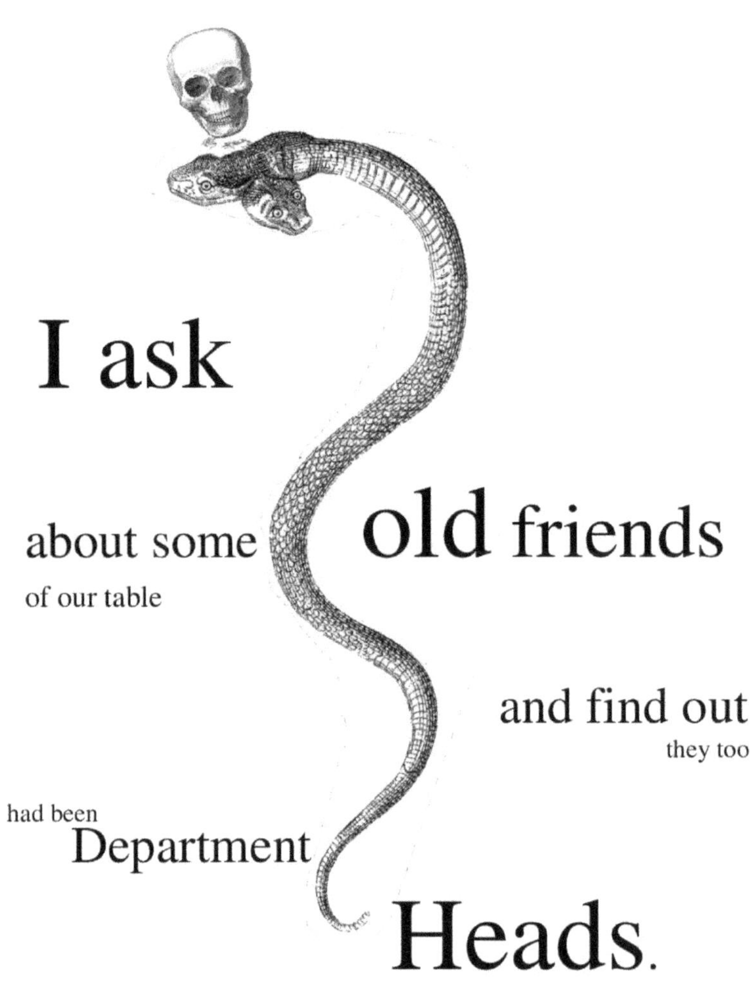

I ask

about some old friends
of our table

and find out
they too

had been
Department

Heads.

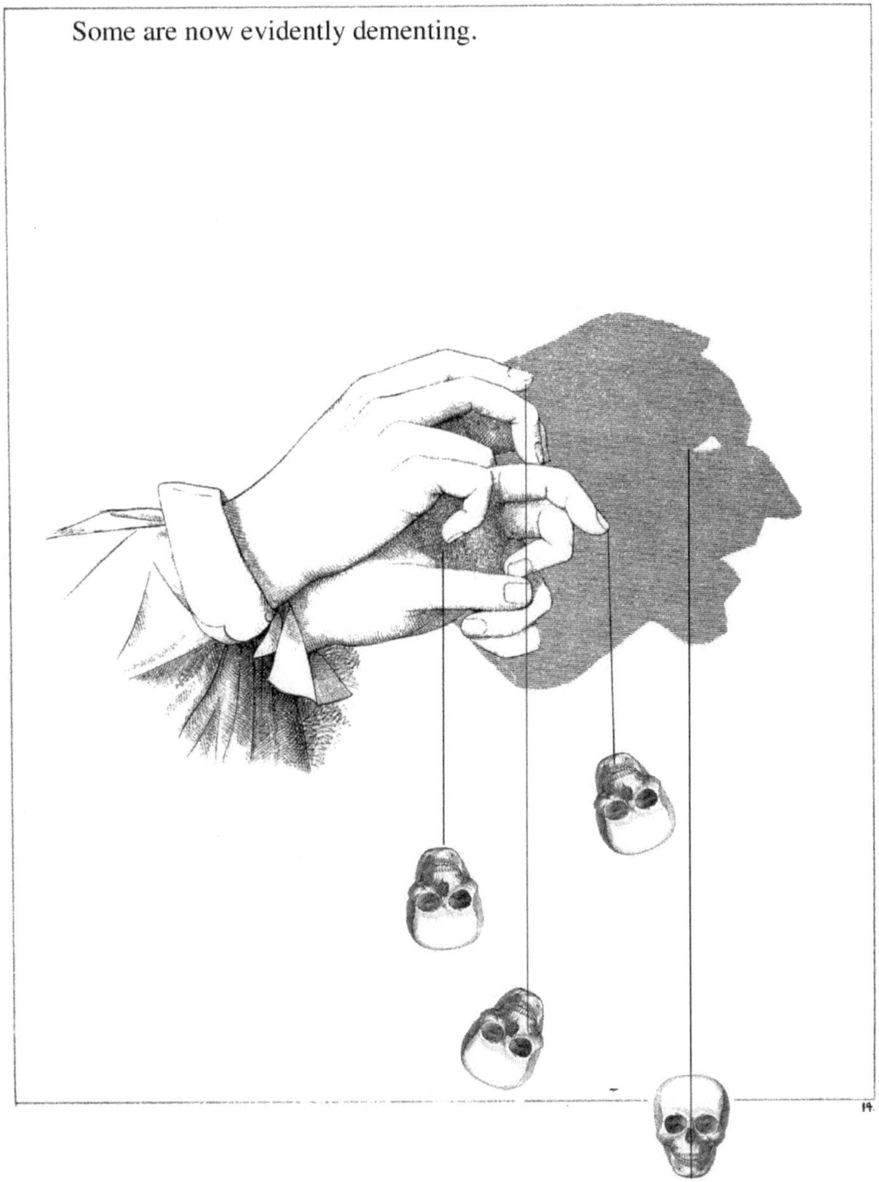

Some are now evidently dementing.

14

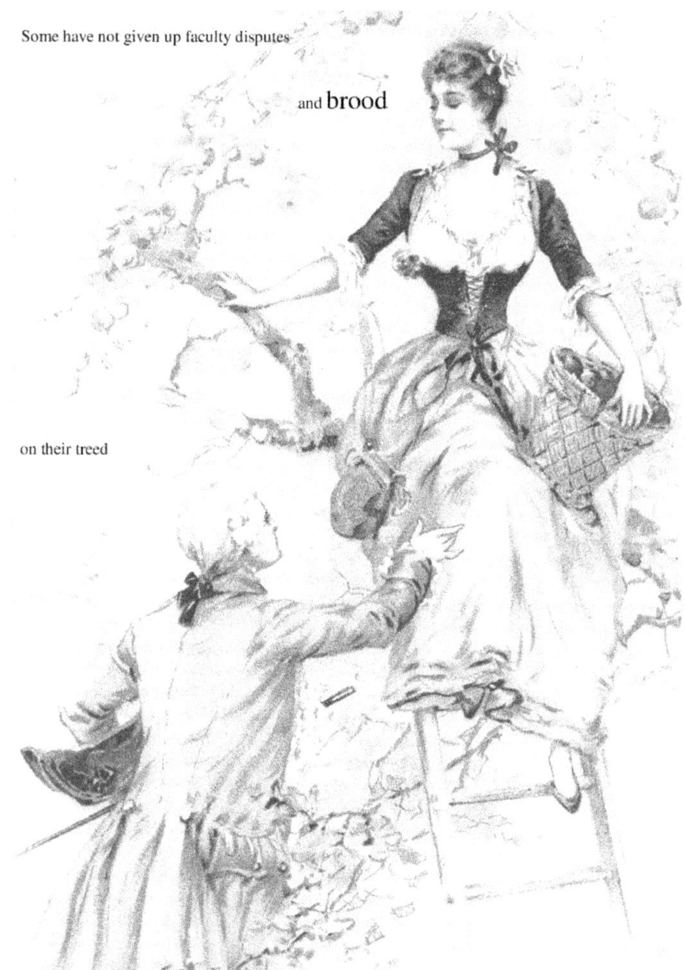

Some have not given up faculty disputes

and brood

on their treed

islands.

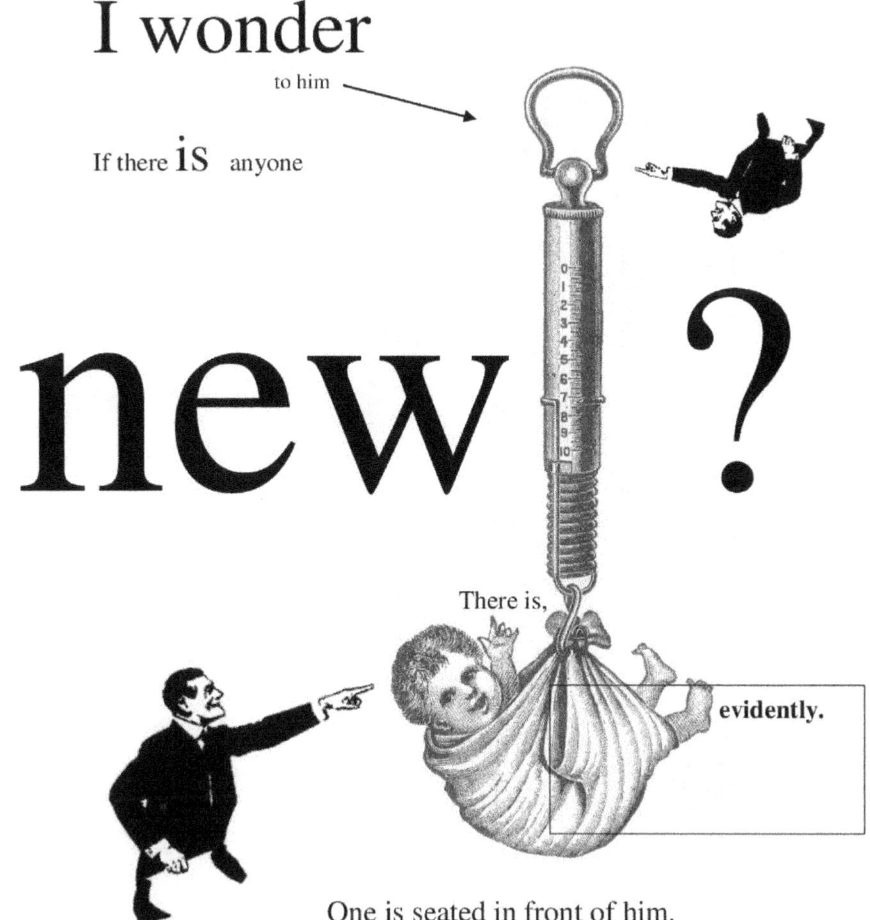
I wonder
to him
If there is anyone
new
?
There is,
evidently.
One is seated in front of him.

He asks **her**

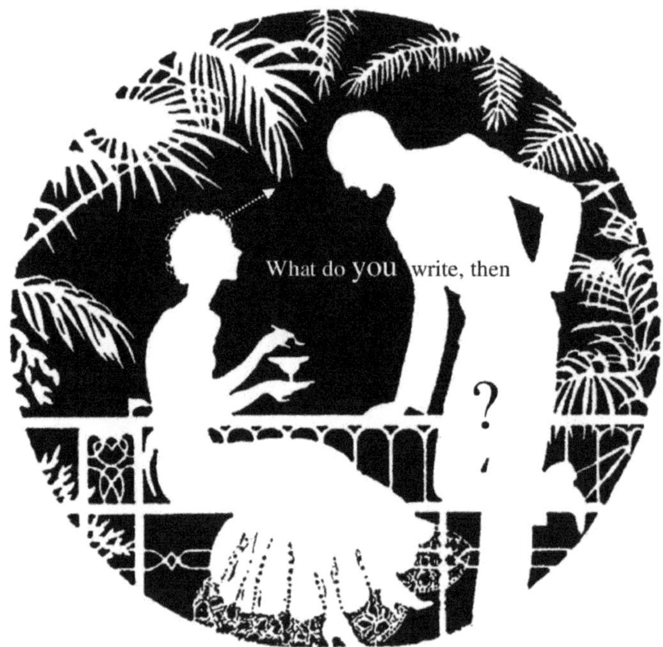

and turns away from me

as I am **not** back.

God bless him.

Now a joke comes to mind

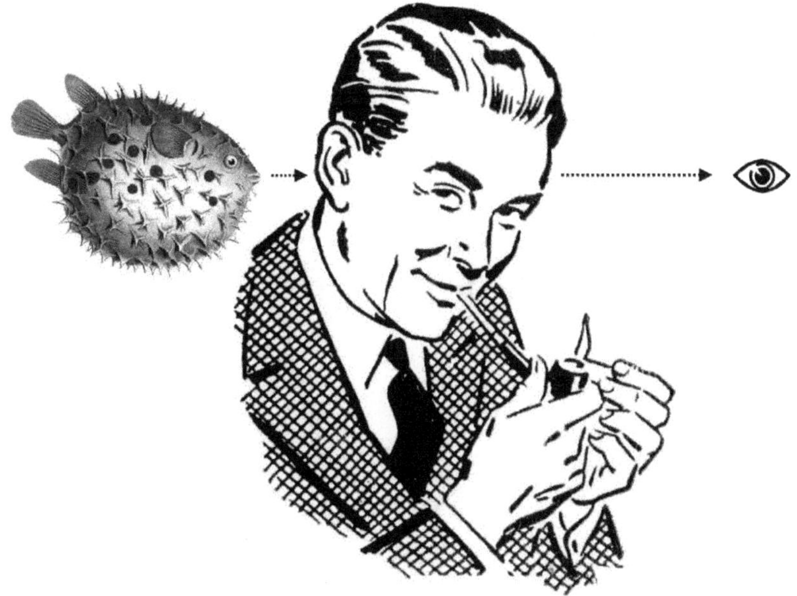

about **Stalin**,

as the coffin is lifted to the hearse.

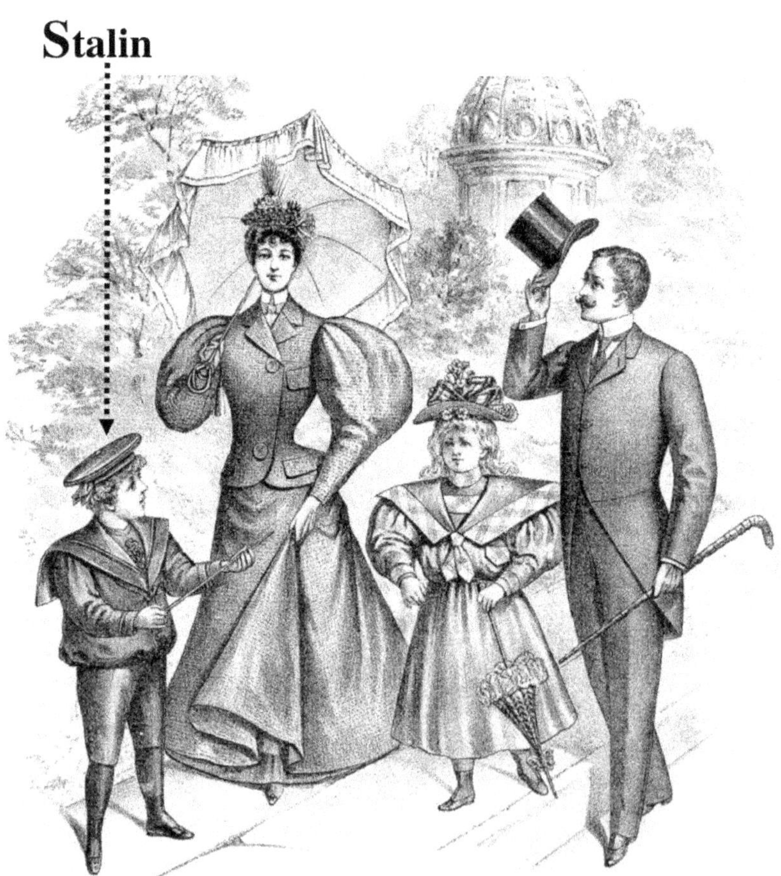

is addressing

an assembly of academics.

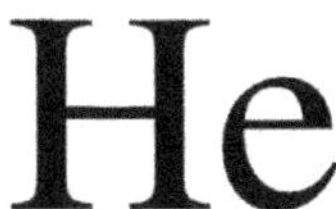

He is talking

traitors

about the tractors to the state

who are propagating ~~right~~ wrong ideology,

the thinking of the

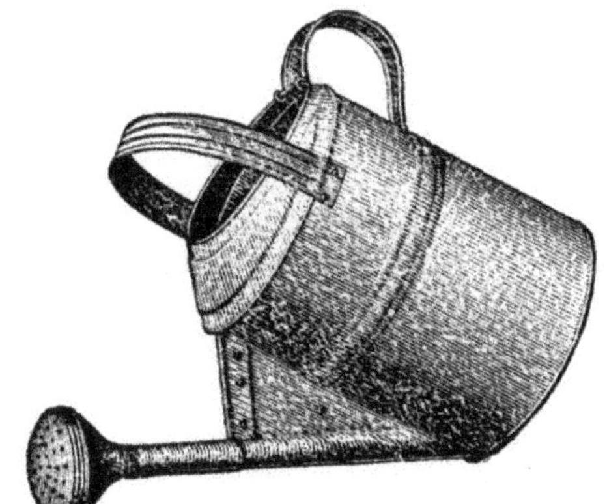

bourgeoisie,

and worse:

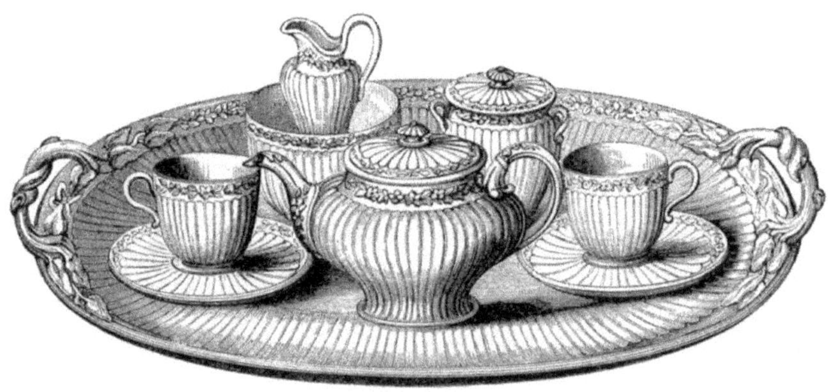

⊠the Trotskyites

and

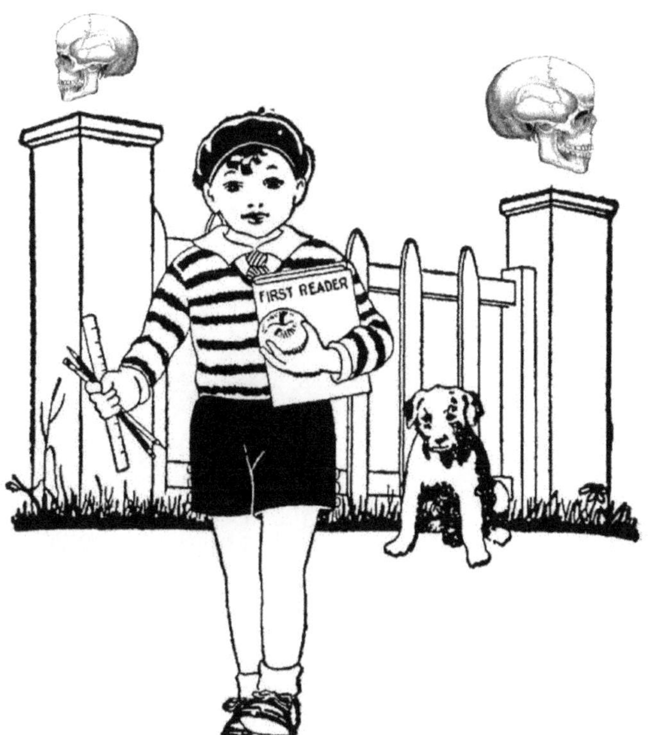

☒ the imperialists.

He is expounding

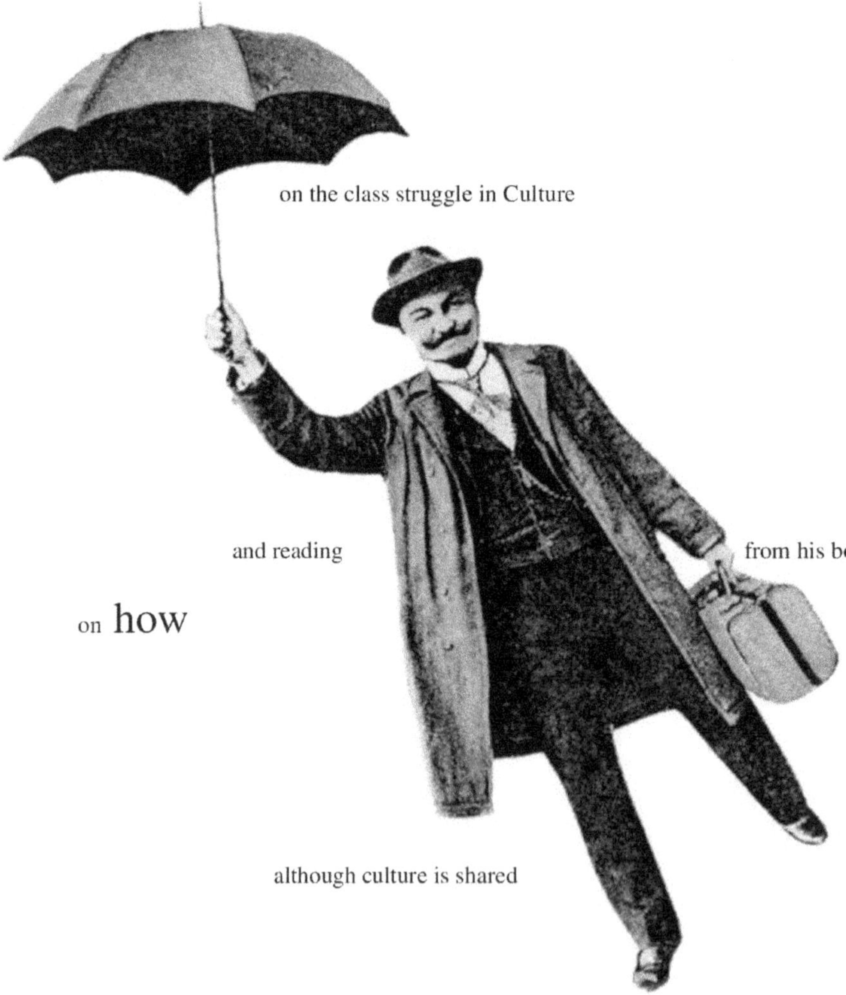

on the class struggle in Culture

and reading

from his book

on how

although culture is shared

by all classes

it is in the service of the working class and

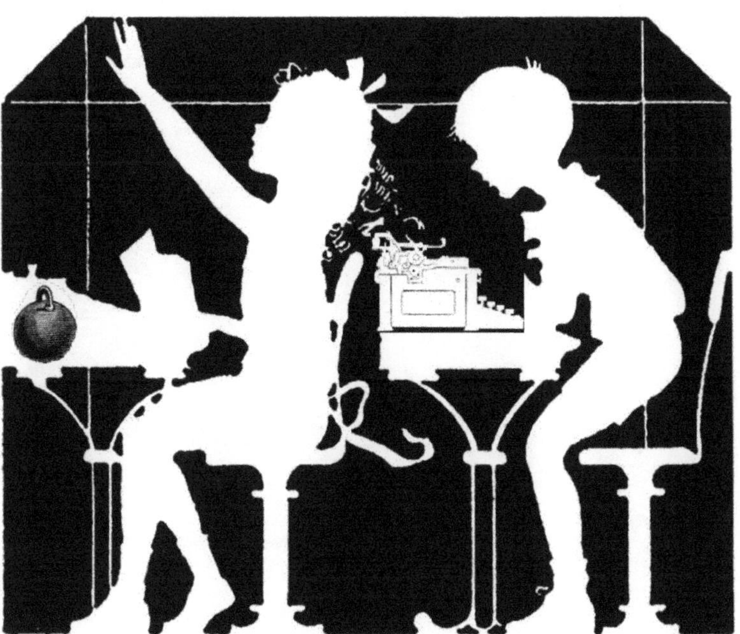

party.

He goes on for two hours

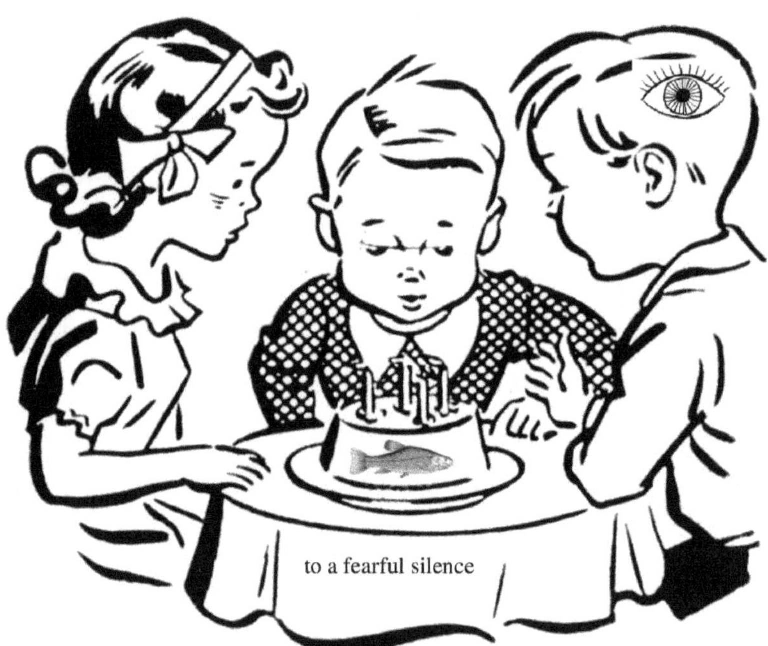

to a fearful silence

in the audience ⋯⋯⋯▸ .

He

explains what the fate will be of those who work against the dictatorship of the proletariat

on the cultural

front.

He pounds the lectern.

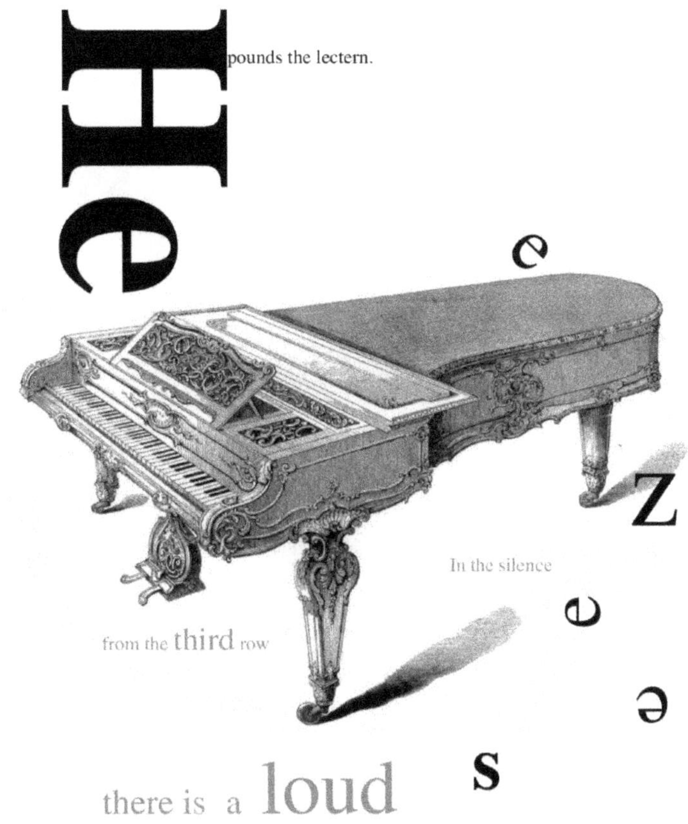

e

Z

In the silence

e

from the third row

e

there is a loud

s

. n

Stalin stops.
There is an even deeper silence.

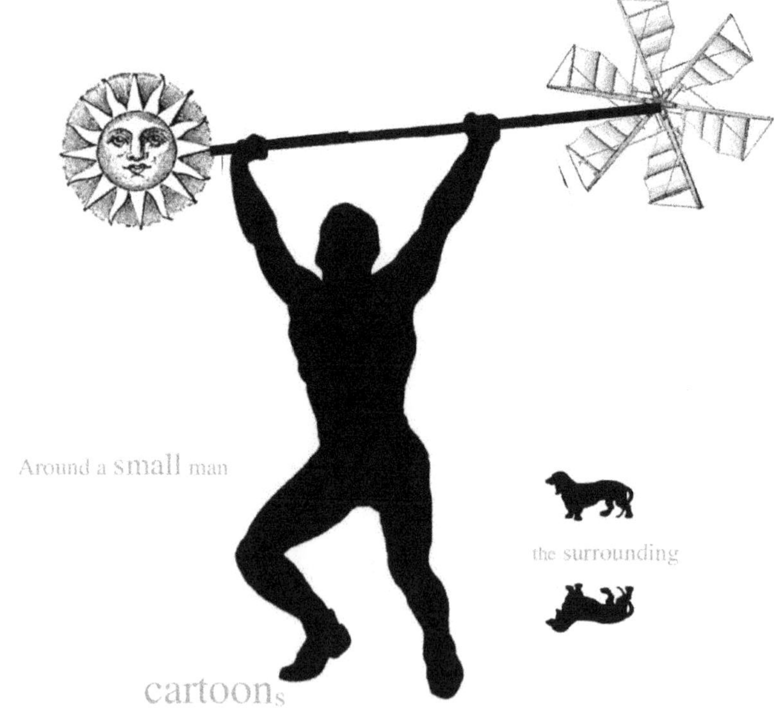

Around a small man

the surrounding

cartoons

angle their bodies to **left**

and rights.

In the row ahead, **cartoons** scrunch down.

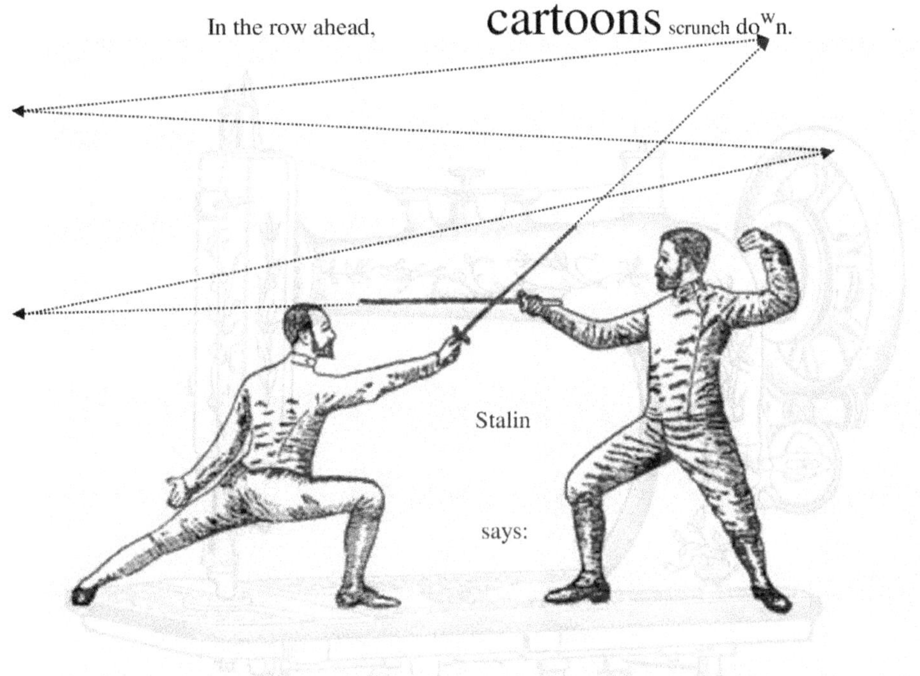

Stalin

says:

'Who sneəzed?'

In the audience there is furtive pointing

like

leaves

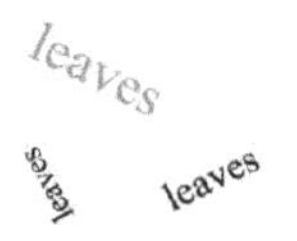

leaves leaves

in a breeze.

The small man looks around.

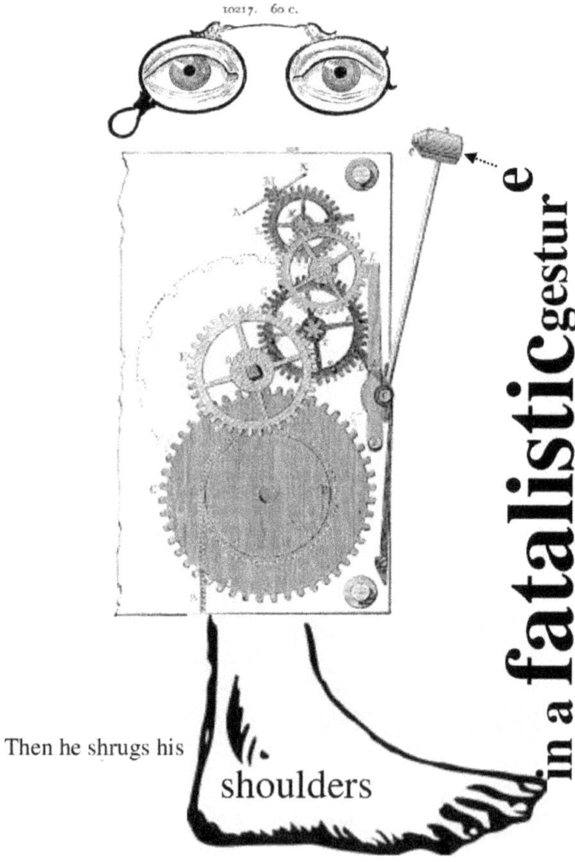

Then he shrugs his shoulders in a fatalistic gesture

and **staring straight**

in his cadre,

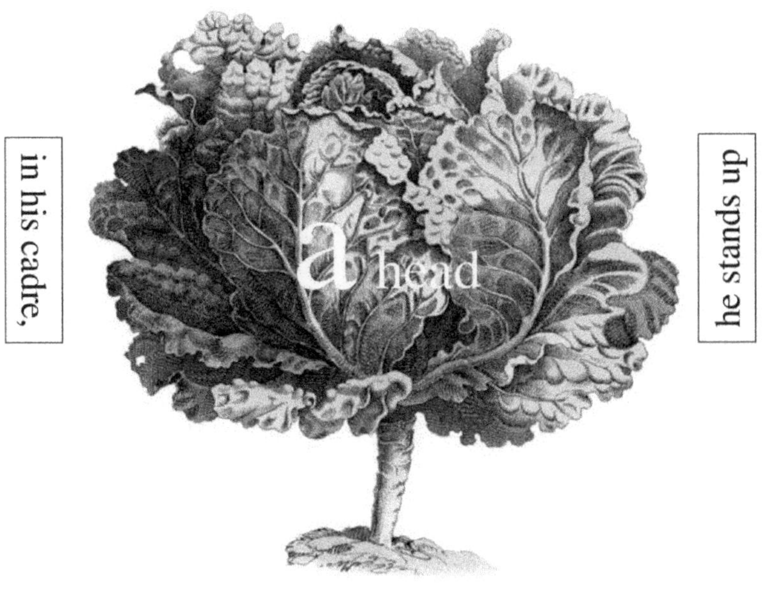

he stands up

— the others already **are** —

where tonight a homeless man is feasting.

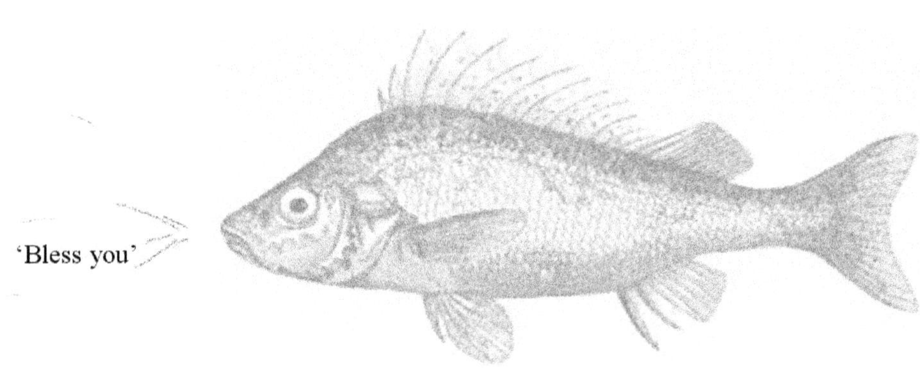

says Stalin.

Goodbye, Robin. Goodbye,

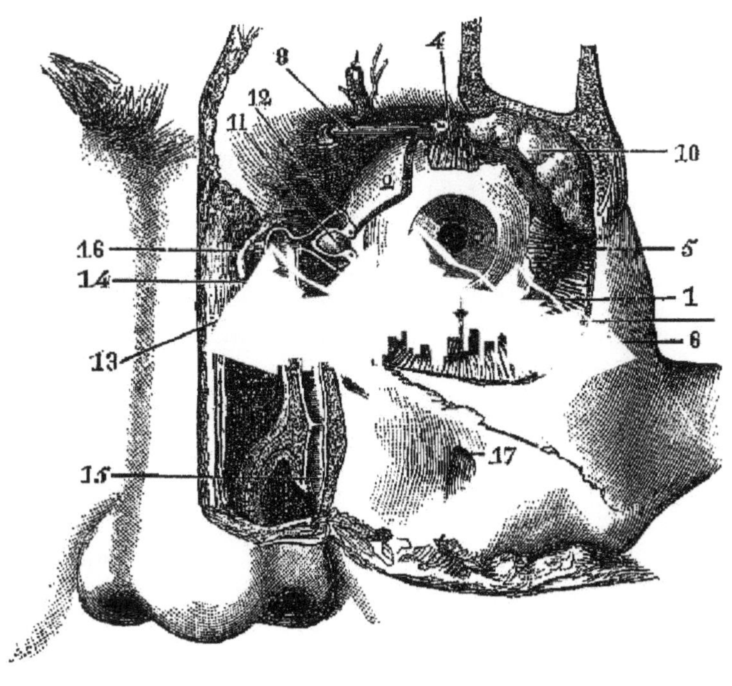

Vancouver.

ABOUT RICHARD RATHWELL

Richard Rathwell is the author of many poems, novels and Facebook series, including the illustrated magazine *Human Nation*. He is a transculturalist, working in literature, aid, trade, and development in difficult situations. As a young activist, he was beaten by a Canadian anti-terrorist unit. Once presumed dead, he was thrown naked into a snowbank and was rescued by a nun. As a project director in West Africa, he channelled funding to the ANC, then underground, and diverted school and cultural centre funds to construct a much-needed mosque. He was expelled from a PhD program for demanding originality. He has exposed corrupt practices in aid and development programs and has been dismissed for it. A friend of a king and a lapsed revolutionary as well as criminals and saints he has been betrayed and lauded without apparent benefit or effect. Many of the schools and hospitals built under his management are now ruins. Many of his agricultural projects are now deserts. His poems and novels continue his practical work. He is currently assisting in the development of independent, transcultural literature and publishing in Africa.

ABOUT HAROLD RHENISCH

Harold Rhenisch is the author of 32 books of poetry, fiction, biography and essays and choreographed Richard Rathwell's *Human Nation* for the paper stage. Along with the Norwegian Olav Hauge, he is one of the two poets in the world who learned to write and edit poems by pruning fruit trees, an experience documented in his *The Tree Whisperer* (Gaspereau, 2021). In 1975, he was typecast as Puck in *A Midsummer Night's Dream*. In 2008, he travelled the Northern Camino, and had to return two years later to rescue himself after discovering that the East German Green Man and had come home in his place. A direct heir of Bertolt Brecht's theater, through the dissident playwright and novelist Stefan Schütz, whose radio play *Peyote* he translated and published, he has invented a theatrical set of cross-genre literary interventions. He has secretly edited and mentored over a hundred writers in the hinterlands of Canada unserved by its university and publishing system and is currently writing a transcultural natural history curriculum and a history of British Columbia centred in the Indian Wars of the American West.

www.ingramcontent.com/pod-product-compliance
Lightning Source LLC
LaVergne TN
LVHW060618110826
845147LV00019B/1043